SO-ALB-345

a B.a.B.e.

*Alyssa ~ Shine for Jesus! Andrea Stephens*

# GIRLFRIEND
## You are a B.a.B.e.!

Beautiful, Accepted, Blessed,
Eternally Significant ™

## andrea stephens

Andrea Stephens
Ministries

© 2005 by Andrea Stephens

Second printing, August 2010

Andrea Stephens Ministries
P.O. Box 75
Fort Myers, FL 33902

Printed in the United States of America

All rights reserved. No part of this publication may be reproduced, stored in a retrieval system, or transmitted in any form or by any means—for example, electronic, photocopy, recording—without the prior written permission of the publisher. The only exception is brief quotations in printed reviews.

Library of Congress had cataloged the original edition of this work as follows.
Stephens, Andrea.
    Girlfriend, you are a B.A.B.E.! : beautiful, accepted, blessed, eternally significant / Andrea Stephens.
        p.     cm.
    ISBN: 978-0-615-39121-2
    1. Teenage girls—Religious life—Juvenile literature.  2. Self-esteem—Religious aspects—Christianity—Juvenile literature.  I. Title.
    BV4551.3.S735  2005
    248.8'33—dc22                                             2005004668

Scripture marked KJV is taken from the King James Version of the Bible.

Scripture marked Message is taken from *The Message* by Eugene H. Peterson, copyright © 1993, 1994, 1995, 2000, 2001, 2002. Used by permission of NavPress Publishing Group. All rights reserved.

Scripture marked NASB is taken from the New American Standard Bible®, Copyright © 1960, 1962, 1963, 1968, 1971, 1972, 1973, 1975, 1977, 1995 by The Lockman Foundation. Used by permission.

Scripture marked NIV is taken from the HOLY BIBLE, NEW INTERNATIONAL VERSION®. NIV®. Copyright © 1973, 1978, 1984 by International Bible Society. Used by permission of Zondervan. All rights reserved.

Scripture marked NLT is taken from the *Holy Bible*, New Living Translation, copyright © 1996. Used by permission of Tyndale House Publishers, Inc., Wheaton, Illinois 60189. All rights reserved.

Scripture marked TLB is taken from *The Living Bible*, copyright © 1971. Used by permission of Tyndale House Publishers, Inc., Wheaton, Illinois 60189. All rights reserved.

The B.A.B.E. Event: Beautiful, Accepted, Blessed, Eternally Significant® is a registered trademark of Andrea Stephens Ministries.

Andrea Stephens Ministries is a non profit 501(c)3 corporation.  All gifts to this ministry are tax-deduxtible and can be given through www.andreastephens.com/ partner.html or sent to P.O. Box 75, Fort Myers, FL 33902.  Thank you for investing in the lives of teen girls.

INTERIOR DESIGN BY BRIAN BRUNSTING

To Allison.

Always missed. Never forgotten.
You are responsible for The B.A.B.E. Event™.
Your encouragement to me has helped
thousands of teen girls understand how precious
and valuable they are to our heavenly Father.
And so many of them have said yes to Jesus, inviting him
into their lives to be their Savior and choosing
to make him their Lord.
I am eternally grateful.
See you when I get there!

# Hey B.a.B.e.!

· · · · · · · · · · ·

Thanks! You Rock!

The B.A.B.E. Journey

*section one*
## B IS FOR BeaUTIFUL!

The Reflection • Beauty and the Beach • Delightfully Designed • Created by the Creator • Masterfully Made: The Amy Carmichael Story • Content Creations • Beauty Obsessed? Take This Quiz! • The Girl Who's Got It All • Digital's Wonderful World of Magic • Now You See It, Now You Don't • The Perfect Body • Flawed or Flawless • When I Look in the Mirror: The Natalie Lloyd Story • Extreme Makeover • Stamp of Approval • Inside Edition: Behind the Scenes with Professional Model Laura Krauss Calenberg • Redefining Beautiful • God-Beauty • Blind Beauty: The Ginny Owens Story • One Hot Divine Diva • The B.A.B.E. Checklist

*section two*
## A IS FOR ACCePTeD!

Wanting to Be Wanted: Heidi's Story • Because You're Worth It • I Choose You! • Whose You Are • eBay Buys • Catching On? • What? No Applause? • A New Audience • Drastic Measures • Two Thumbs Up • Sitting Pretty • Who You Are in Christ • Frapuccino Flops • But I Don't *Feel* It! • Raunchy Rejection • Blast Out the Blues • Weeds • Sorting through the Voices • Your View of You • The Good, the Bad, and the Ugly • Courageously Confident • The B.A.B.E. Checklist

• • • *Check out what's inside!*

*section three*
## B IS FOR BLESSED!

Blessed? It Means, Umm . . .
• A Different Kind of Blessing
• Spiritual Blessings • Spirit
Power: The Real Deal •
Precious Fruit • Inside Edition:
True Fruit with Joy Williams •
Gifts Galore • What Flavor Is
Yours? • Just the Facts, Please
• Defining Moments • Lights,
Camera, Action • What's
in Your Gift Box? • Taking
Stock of Your Spiritual Gifts •
Dancing in the Rain • Naturally
You! • Kaleidoscope Blessings •
Strike Three, You're Out: The
Alese Coco Story • Hugs from
Heaven • The Blessings Book •
The B.A.B.E. Checklist

*section four*
## E IS FOR ETERNALLY SIGNIFICANT!

No Expiration Date • Nothing
to It? • You Matter! • Star
Light, Star Bright • Inside
Edition: Campus Alert! The
Bible Comes to School •
Significantly Successful •
More than a Clay Lump • I
Want to Be A . . . • All about
Me • All about Him • Life
Scripts • The General Cast •
The Starring Role • Playing
Your Part • Endless Options
• Every Day Is Eternity • Prep
Time • Ad Libs • Encore! •
Roll the Credits • This Is God's
Deal: The BarlowGirl Story •
BarlowBeliefs • Curtain Call
• Lordship Countdown • The
Unending Adventure • The
B.A.B.E. Checklist

*Shine Like a B.A.B.E.!*
It's a Wrap! • Catch the
B.A.B.E. Wave • Be a
B.A.B.E. in Action! The
Ultimate Spa Experience • The
B.A.B.E. "Chat It Up" Guide
• The B.A.B.E. "Chat It Up"
Leader's Guide

# *Thanks!*
# YOU ROCK!

The completion of a writing project (especially a series) marks the beginning of expressing my gratitude and heartfelt appreciation for those who have contributed, supported, prayed for, edited, and critiqued this work. Wow. I sound so formal! I really just want to say, "Hey, thanks a ton. You mean so much to me!"

The B.A.B.E. series is my heart. It is what my ministry is all about. It is one of the eternally significant assignments God has given to me. It uses the gifts and talents with which he has so generously blessed me. I'm both honored and humbled for the time, talent, energy, and love each of you has given to make this assignment more awesome and more fun. I'm grateful that you care about me personally, but more so, that you care about teen girls.

To Alive Communications for convincing me I had a few more youth books still in me.

To Suzette for your diligent research, editing, and contributions. You amaze me!

To Carol for giving your unmatched expertise. You've blessed me!

To Nell for picking up the slack behind the scenes. How did I get so lucky?

To Francie for your precious prayers and your patience when I needed to vent. You're a saint!

To Ann, Lisa, Tracie, and Nancy for helping to keep The B.A.B.E. Seminar™ under control while I've been busy writing! I'm thankful to be a recipient of your gifts of service!

To Mom and Dad (R.J. and Joanne Ardner) for supporting me at the seminars and helping with The B.A.B.E. MiniMag. Your tireless work done with love and patience is a great example to me! I love you.

To the Roberts, the Spellmans, and the O'Briens. Your encouragement and feedback means everything!

To Katie, Karlee, Kali, and Cassidy for being my inspiration.

To Katie Sherrill for your insightful reading of the manuscript from a youth worker's perspective. You were so helpful!

To all of my prayer partners for lifting me up to the throne room.

To the friendly and efficient waitresses at Pappy's and Spencer's. You've never even asked my name, but you've kept my coffee cup full and allowed me to get lost in my thoughts until I realized I was hungry and needed some breakfast!

And finally, to Bill for loving me in spite of my messiness and for helping me keep my eye on the big picture. You're a great partner in Christ! I love you!

May all glory go to God. He alone is my reason.

# THE B.A.B.E. JOURNEY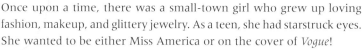

Once upon a time, there was a small-town girl who grew up loving fashion, makeup, and glittery jewelry. As a teen, she had starstruck eyes. She wanted to be either Miss America or on the cover of *Vogue*!

Okay, this isn't really a fairy tale. It's my life.

I went for the pageant thing first. I polished up my classical guitar performance, worked hard to get straight A's, read up on current events, and entered the Junior Miss Scholarship Program. I finished second in the state pageant. A few years later, I entered the Miss Oklahoma Pageant. Second again! Therefore, not being a state winner with obligations, I switched gears and prepared for a modeling convention later that summer. Well, the Miss America dream went on hold, because the trip to New York City won me a contract with Wilhelmina Models, Inc.

I was thrilled. I packed my bags and moved to the city a few weeks later.

Lights, camera, action! I was ready. I settled into a small apartment with several other models, then took to the streets for my go-sees (that's model talk for the word *interview*, you'd go see if you were the right person for the job) and photo shoots.

I learned quickly that ad agents and photographers have no problem telling you if they don't like your appearance. "We're searching for someone with a different look." Or "The end of your nose is too rounded." Or "We don't like the way your neck curves or the size of your teeth or the way your hair moves." Really, nothing was off limits for these people! And how unfair to be compared to retouched perfection.

After a while, I noticed I started to feel unsure of myself. It seemed my confidence was slipping away. Questions surfaced. Is this shirt right for me? Is my rear getting big? Does my makeup look good? Is my hair hip enough? How can I look taller? Should I lose weight? Why would anyone want to hire me? Should I get this mole on my cheek removed? Do I have enough money for breast implants?

Even though in the short time I had been in New York I had landed a national commercial, been on several magazine covers, and had a handful of catalog jobs, it wasn't enough to offset the negative comments and the comparisons. My sensitive nature soaked them right in. I felt that almost everything about me was wrong. Inadequate. Not good enough.

At the same time, God was using my modeling experience to show me that he had a different plan for my life, a plan that would amount to more than just having my smiling face promoting a product or gracing a magazine cover. This was something that would be much bigger than a supermodel or an A-list actor. It would be a plan that would have heart—his heart!

It was time to move home.

Yet it seemed to be the worst possible timing. I had just finished my composite card, and I was about to be officially introduced to the market in the *Wilhelmina Models* book.

My roommates thought I was crazy.

"What could be more important than attaining superstar status or making some big bucks?" they argued. "Besides, you're signed with a great agency, you're working with a famous acting coach, and your vocal trainer's the best." They almost had me convinced. But as I watched one light up a joint, one mix a drink, and one pop her birth control pill, it just confirmed my inner conviction that God wanted something better for me.

The second week after I moved home, I was handed information about a one-year Bible training program. I knew it was for me. Though I had been a believer since I was young, I had never really studied the

Bible. In fact, I didn't get my first Bible until I was sixteen. Since my future was going to be about God's plans for me, knowing his Word was core. Yet little did I know that this would change my life most dramatically.

As I studied the Bible, I discovered many verses that explained God's view and opinion of me. I found out he created and designed me in a way that delighted him. To him, I was **beautiful**. I learned that I didn't have to look or act perfect for him to love and approve of me. He **accepted** me. And he gave me talents and spiritual gifts that he wanted me to develop so I could use them to serve him. Indeed, I was **blessed** by him. And about that plan I mentioned earlier, it was starting to play out before my eyes. No flashy stuff that was here today and gone tomorrow. God's plan for me was going to be **eternally significant**.

See, he had to heal my self-esteem (the way I feel about myself) with the truth of his Word before he could call me to help heal yours. Many of the experiences God has taken me through have been part of his preparation to bring me to this point right now.

I've been teaching the truths in this book for years. But for the first time, God has brought them together under the acronym B.A.B.E. I've seen your generation struggle with depression, eating disorders, cutting, alcohol and drug addiction, casual sex, STDs, and hopelessness. I believe these are all symptoms of low self-esteem. They're holding many young women (maybe even you) back from becoming all God has meant for them to be.

Well, not anymore.

Life will change when you finally see yourself the way God sees you. Life will improve when you realize that he created you *on* purpose and *for* a purpose. You will be empowered to blossom when you understand that you are beautiful, accepted, blessed, and eternally significant.

Girlfriend, you are a B.A.B.E.! I'm going to prove it to you! It's not based on your looks, feelings, or social status. It's based on the unchanging truth in God's Word.

Let's get started!

Oh, by the way, God calls us to imitate (or model) Jesus. So I *am* still a model. Just a different kind. Isn't God cool?

**1**

**B** IS FOR

# Beau

TIFUL!

# the REFLECTION

"Two-face!"

The words that came spurting out of her friend's mouth left her speechless.

"Sticks and stones may break my bones, but words will never hurt me!" Sarah Kimberlin knew firsthand that this childhood phrase wasn't true.

Words do hurt.

Sarah was born on May 4, 1985, a healthy baby girl. She learned to coo and crawl, wiggle and walk, chatter and giggle, smile and laugh! But soon after she blew out those two big candles on her birthday cake, Sarah's parents noticed that the right side of their toddler's face wasn't developing properly. In fact, the small muscles seemed to be tightening and shriveling. After many frantic trips in and out of doctors' offices, Sarah's parents were told she had a brain tumor. Wanting a second opinion, they took their small daughter to the University of California San Francisco Medical Center, where an accurate diagnosis was made.

Sarah had been struck with Parry-Romberg syndrome, a muscle disorder that caused atrophy in one side of the face. The muscle tissue not only stopped growing, but eventually disappeared. She became the youngest documented case of Parry-Romberg syndrome in the world.

While Sarah was growing up, her parents taught her that she wasn't really any different than anyone else. She could play and run and read just like the other kids. She loved science and art. It was just her facial muscles that were unique.

Yes, kids at school gave her guff and sometimes left her out. Yes, she caught people staring at her. But Sarah's mom and dad helped her choose not to believe what anyone else said or did, but instead to focus on the bigger picture. God must have a plan. Certainly he would use this situation in a positive way.

Over the years, sinus infections and breathing difficulties plagued Sarah. So due to a severely deviated septum in her nose (caused by the Parry-Romberg), Sarah had reconstructive surgery the summer before her sophomore year in high school. (A deviated septum is a condition where the wall that separates the nose into two nasal passages becomes crooked, thus blocking the passages.) During complex surgery, a piece of Sarah's right ear was used to build up the side of her nose, and a piece of bone removed from one of her ribs built up the brow bone around her eye. Eight hours and over six hundred stitches later, Sarah was wheeled into the recovery room. Hours later she was breathing normally for the first time since she was a toddler.

To the doctors, this was the first phase of their plan for Sarah. To Sarah, it was the last.

When given the option for further surgery—this time with the goal of mirroring the right side of her face to the left—Sarah refused. The two sides of her face didn't match. One eye drooped. Her right cheekbone was nonexistent. Yet she didn't want to change a thing.

Sarah's classmates couldn't understand how she could look so different yet be so confident. How could she like her look when they didn't like theirs?

But when Sarah gazed into the bathroom mirror, she didn't see **different**. She didn't see unattractive. She didn't see ugly. When she looked at her reflection, she didn't see odd.

She saw special.
One of a kind.
Really? Yep, really!
Even with the teasing? The blank stares? The offhanded remarks?
Yep. **How could this be?**
Sarah had come to understand something that changed her life. As she read the Bible, she saw that God doesn't look at things like we do. Sarah understood that in God's eyes she was beautiful. She knew that when God looked at her, he saw a young woman he had handcrafted, a young woman who was shining from the confidence of his love.
To God, she was gorgeous.
To Sarah, that was **all** that mattered.
**The B in B.A.B.E. is for beautiful!**
Beautiful, that's you!

## In Her Own Words . . .

Everyone is attractive in their own way! Maybe the star football player doesn't see it, but that does not matter. You *can* love yourself, and you *have* to love yourself! Triumph in being the unique young woman whom God made very special!

~ Sarah Kimberlin

# BeaUTY anD THe BeaCH

I don't know, maybe it's because I grew up in the Midwest. Maybe it's because I never saw it live and in person until I was nearly twenty years old. Maybe it's because the vastness of it causes me to sense the presence of the one who created it.

Whatever the reason, the fact remains.

I **love** the ocean!

I'm a total beach woman!

The moment I laid my dark green eyes on its aqua blue water, its pure white waves, and its sandy beige beaches, the ocean captured my heart.

Have you been to the ocean? Have you seen the big blue sea?

Perhaps you feel the same way. Maybe you love all the cool things you can do in the water, like body surf, swim, sail, or ride the WaveRunner.

All that stuff's fun, but by far my favorite thing to do at the beach (besides deepen my "fake-bake tan") is to stroll along the shoreline. It's the ultimate. Okay, it might not sound very thrilling to you, but hang tight and I'll explain my passion!

Over the years I've been fortunate to have left my footprints on many beaches. As I've walked the various shorelines, feeling their sand between my toes, I've loved watching the waves. I'm fascinated at the way they rise, crest, rush up toward the sand, and then calmly pull back out to sea. And I've discovered something. On nearly every beach I've strolled, the ocean has left pieces of itself behind.

Like little gifts from the sea, nestled there in the sand, are portions of the ocean's contents. Contents I've been collecting for years.

Have you figured it out?

Shells!

So many shapes! So many sizes! So many colors! So many patterns and so many textures!

For example, the long spiral shell with the pointed tip I discovered washed up on the shore of the Indian Ocean while I was on a mission trip in Africa. And the fan-shaped orange shell with a slanted edge, and the teeny-tiny purple one that was washed up from the Gulf of Mexico. Then there's the short, round shell with a natural shine that came home in my suitcase from Hawaii! (In Hawaii nearly every shell I saw was moving. It was attached to the back of a big slug, a snail. It was something's home. Now, I just couldn't bring myself to steal some poor slug's house off its back, so I actually prayed that God would allow me to find just one empty house—I mean shell—so I could take it home. He did. Sweet, huh?)

Each shell is unique; no two of them are **exactly** alike.

God made them all, and he made all of them different!

Well, one day I was thinking.

What if someone came along and declared to the world that the fan-shaped orange shell with the slanted edge was the most beautiful shell? And what if he or she declared that from now on the attractiveness of all the other shells would be judged by whether or not they looked like this one fan-shaped orange shell?

Uh-oh!

What about the purple shell I love, or the cool spiral one?

What about the rounded one from aloha land?

If only one shell was declared gorgeous, then I have collected a whole bunch of really ugly shells, because none of the other shells look exactly like the one that was deemed beautiful!

Would that be fair? No!

It would be unfair, unrealistic, and not what God intended. (He happens to think all of his creations are pretty darn unique and great looking.)

# DELIGHTFULLY DESIGNED

But wait.

Isn't this exactly what happens to us?

God has designed each of us different. We are unique. Individual.

Then our culture comes along and declares that this one particular image is the perfect and most beautiful image and that if we do not measure up to that exalted image, we are not attractive.

That is unfair, unrealistic, and not at all what God intended!

That's exactly what the media dishes out. Our culture has an unre-

> **You have a beauty all your own.**

alistic beauty standard that has been created by the media—you know, the guys with the big businesses who try to get you to buy their products!

Let's see how tuned-in you are. Circle the features on this list that you think are part of this beauty standard:

- a pear-shaped body
- zit-free skin
- high cheekbones
- yellow teeth
- moles and birthmarks
- toned muscles
- thick, bouncy hair
- short fingernails
- long eyelashes
- almond-shaped eyes
- bushy eyebrows
- full bustline
- straight nose
- tall, skinny body
- protruding belly
- tight rear

Not too hard, huh?

The entertainment industry, the fashion industry, the music industry, the modeling and acting industries have reinforced this beauty standard. They hold this standard up and judge females' beauty based on how close they come to resembling the chick in the photo.

And the judging spreads.

Candace sat staring into the rearview mirror at her high forehead. She tried to hide it under her bangs, but bangs were so yesterday, and a booming forehead was so gross. "At least I don't have a huge pebble-looking mole protruding off my chin like Misty does. Nobody would want that obnoxious thing," she snidely whispered to herself.

See what happens?

We begin to judge the attractiveness of ourselves and others based on our culture's unrealistic standard.

Unfair! Unrealistic! Not what God intended! (Yes, I know I already said that, but I wanted to say it again just so you wouldn't breeze by it!)

It's been said that beauty is in the eye of the beholder. Well, girl, as God beholds you, as he gazes at you, he sees outrageously gorgeous.

He sees perfectly pretty.

He sees awesomely attractive.

You are **beautiful** in God's eyes!

Why? Why does God think you're beautiful? Because he created and designed you in a way that **delights** him.

Listen in to what King David says to God:

You made all the delicate, inner parts of my body, and knit them together in my mother's womb. Thank you for making me so wonderfully complex! It is amazing to think about. Your workmanship is marvelous—and how well I know it.

Psalm 139:13–14 TLB

Incredible, isn't it? God was there overseeing your conception; he was at work weaving you, forming you, putting you together. You were handcrafted! Knit together by a Master Designer! You were beautifully created. Yes, beautiful! You were molded by loving hands into the shape and size that pleased your Designer's heart.

You are also wonderfully complex. Think about it.

One square inch of skin contains over one billion cells. Your brain has ten thousand million nerve cells. You think over a million thoughts a day. Each of your eyes has millions of rods and cones that enable your eyesight and help you distinguish over four thousand different colors. Your heart pumps over two thousand gallons of blood per day. Your ear has millions of microscopic hairs that send electrical nerve signals to your brain. Your DNA is unlike anyone else's. Your brain has four separate lobes, together weighing three pounds. You have thirty bones in your hand and wrist. Your fifty billion white blood cells attack any invaders who enter into your bloodstream.

Wonderfully complex. David was right. It is amazing to think about it!

Yep, delightfully designed! That's you!

# CREATED BY THE CREATOR

Let these words from the Bible cut through the rubble of inaccurate teaching, modern philosophies, and the reasoning of mere man that you've heard floating around. Allow them to solidify in your heart what is absolutely true—you were created by God!

"In the beginning God created the heavens and the earth." ~ Genesis 1:1 NLT

"When I look up into the night skies and see the work of your fingers—the moon and the stars you have made—I cannot understand how you can bother with mere puny man, to pay attention to him! And yet you have made him only a little lower than the angels, and place a crown of glory and honor upon his head."
~ Psalm 8:3–5 TLB

"So God created people in his own image; God patterned them after himself; male and female he created them." ~ Genesis 1:27 NLT

"And the LORD God formed a man's body from the dust of the ground and breathed into it the breath of life. And the man became a living person."
~ Genesis 2:7 NLT

"But now, O Israel, the LORD who created you says: . . . 'I have called you by name; you are mine. . . . You are precious to me . . . and I love you. . . . For I have made them for my glory. . . . It was

> **Don't allow anyone's words or actions keep you from seeing your true God-given beauty.**

I who created them.'"
~ Isaiah 43:1–7 NLT

"God, the LORD, created the heavens and stretched them out. He created the earth and everything in it. He gives breath and life to everyone in all the world." ~ Isaiah 42:5 NLT

"We are the clay, and you are the potter. We are all formed by your hand."
~ Isaiah 64:8 NLT

"Acknowledge that the LORD is God! He made us, and we are his." ~ Psalm 100:3 NLT

"Before I formed you in the womb I knew you."
~ Jeremiah 1:5 NASB

"Christ is the one through whom God created everything in heaven and earth. He made the things we can see and the things we can't see." ~ Colossians 1:16 NLT

Based on the Bible, mark the following statements that are true.

____ You have been patterned after God's image.
____ Some things evolved naturally and were not created.
____ You were created for God's glory.

____ God gave you life and breath.

____ God is your personal potter.

____ God knew you before you were even born.

It's called being "custom designed." An original. If you have ever watched the *Oscars* or the *Golden Globe Awards*, then you know that the dazzling dresses draping the frames of the female stars who are up for the coveted awards are always designer originals. And after those dresses are worn that one time, they're often sold to collectors or museums at exorbitantly high prices. Why? Because there are no other gowns just like them. Each one is a one-of-a-kind design. Individual. Never to be repeated. **Just like you!**

I hope you're getting excited about yourself! You're definitely not a carbon copy or a clone. You can learn to love and appreciate your unique design. Please don't let someone's playful joke, cruel comment, or tactless teasing keep you from seeing your true God-given beauty.

In case you were wondering, rest assured that when you were being constructed, you weren't haphazardly thrown together. You were designed with a purpose! Just the way God intended!

## Masterfully Made:
# THE AMY CARMICHAEL STORY

As a young girl, Amy Carmichael peered into the bathroom mirror at her big brown eyes and wished they were blue.

That morning at the breakfast table, she asked her mother the question that had plagued her. "Mother, do you think God can change the color of my eyes?"

Amy's very wise mom responded to her daughter, saying, "Amy, God can do anything he wants to do."

So Amy decided to ask him! She prayed very hard that night, asking God to change her big brown eyes to baby blues. Then she went to bed. She was so excited she could barely sleep.

The next morning Amy shot out of bed, ran to the bathroom, and looked into the mirror with great expectation.

Guess what happened.

Nothing!

There were those big brown eyes looking right back at her.

At first Amy was miffed (as in totally ticked) at God.

She didn't understand why he chose not to grant her request. Was it too much for him? Was it too hard for him? Why was he not willing?

Amy took her brown eyes and her downcast spirit to her mother. After listening to her daughter's outburst of questions, Amy's loving mother gave her a reassuring reply. "Amy, God must have a plan for you and those big brown eyes."

Little did her mom know how true her words would prove to be!

Amy Carmichael was born December 16, 1867, in the village of Millisle on the northern coast of Ireland. She was raised in a devout Christian family and fell in love with Jesus at an early age.

As a teen, Amy had an experience that proved to be a defining moment.

One Sunday afternoon on the way home from church, Amy and her brothers came upon a frail woman who was all bent over carrying a heavy bundle. Several members of Amy's church had passed by, seeing the poor woman, but hadn't stopped to help. Amy was furious. The self-righteous attitude of her fellow church members was unacceptable to her. With her brothers' help, Amy took the woman's bundle and walked her into town.

In her heart Amy knew what really mattered in life. She said, "Nothing could ever matter again but the things that were eternal." The things that had lasting value.

Amy was serious about that. She made the choice to serve God with her life.

On January 13, 1892, God called Amy Carmichael to be a missionary to India.

Dressed like a native, with a veil across her face, Amy would sneak into the Hindu temples and rescue young girls who had been forced into a life of prostitution. Dressed in that garb, she wasn't recognized. In fact, all that could be seen were those big brown eyes! The eyes that were the same color as the native women's!

Amy established orphanages where the young girls were graciously cared for and were told of the saving love of God's Son, Jesus.

Think of it. If Amy Carmichael had been created with blue eyes, she would have been recognized and arrested! God couldn't have used her to save hundreds of children from a horrible life!

God gave Amy big brown eyes on purpose! He designed her just the way he wanted. He did the same with you! And he did a great job! He loves what you see when you look in the mirror! You are beautiful in God's eyes!*

*Did you know missionary Amy Carmichael was also a poet and hymn writer? Get all the details in *Amy Carmichael* by Kathleen White (published by Bethany House).

# Content CREATIONS

Remember David's comments in Psalm 139:13–14? (See page 18.) Allow me to draw your attention to an astounding statement. Take a look back at the first two words of the second sentence. Do you see them? Are you shocked? David, known to be one of the greatest men in history, said thank you to his Creator. **Thank you!** Perhaps this was a key to his greatness. David was content with the way God made him. There is no record of him spewing complaints and criticisms to his Maker for doing a lousy job.

Okay, I'll be the first to admit that I used to be guilty of griping, especially when I was strutting down runways, vying for crowns, or prepping for photo shoots. Rather than seeing everything that was right about me, I focused on everything I thought was wrong. For instance, forget five foot seven; I wanted to be five foot nine. I wanted thicker hair that was ultrashiny. I wanted my breasts to be bigger. (Hold on. I have a *lot* more to say about a woman's chest later.) I thought I'd be happier if my nose was a little less rounded, if my hips were a bit smaller, if my eyelashes were just a tad longer. What must God think when we do that?

I hear girls (and women) constantly complaining about their looks, their bodies. They don't like their hips, their thighs, their rears, their waistlines, their knees, their teeth, their ears, their freckles, their lips. It's endless. It's ungrateful.

Naturally, your look will change as your body completes the puberty process. Some of those features that have been harder to be thankful for may be temporary. Perhaps your most picked-on features will become your most prized possessions. It happened for me as my pitifully sticklike legs with knobby knees won me the preliminary swimsuit competition and a college scholar-ship in the Miss Oklahoma Pageant! Fact is, most girls aren't supermodel material based on our world's unrealistic beauty standard. But every girl—yes, even you—is a work of art, fear-fully and wonderfully made by a loving Designer. Appreciate your special features and trust his wisdom as you grow into the final you! Love your look, because it's from the Lord!

Here's an idea. How 'bout we put a new spin on this—in the **opposite** direction? How 'bout we throw our thoughts in reverse? How 'bout we do a 180 and begin to thank God for the **fact** that he designed us and the **way** that he designed us? Especially those parts you wish you could change! Embrace them!

Go ahead. Start now. It may just give you a fresh perspec-tive. It may just cause you to begin to see how lovingly and lovely you have been made. It may just change criticism to **contentment**.

That, my friend, will set your heart free.

That, my friend, will begin to unravel your twisted thinking if you've been wrapped up in this whole unrealistic beauty standard our culture has created.

That is exactly what happened to Heather (not her real name).

I met Heather sitting in an airport in Quito, Ecuador. We were on our way home from a *Brio* mission trip. Heather was headed to Oklahoma; I was headed to California. We'd been on this trip together for fourteen days, but we'd never met until now. As I entered the waiting area, God chose to leave one seat open, the seat next to this petite high school girl whose dyed hair was badly faded. I don't recall how we started talking, but it wasn't long before we were in a full-blown discussion about beauty and looks (okay, being the beauty editor for *Brio* magazine, people tend to get into these types of discussions with me). I recall almost arguing with Heather because I passionately wanted her to understand that she wasn't designed to fit some beauty standard, but instead was already beautiful because that's

Contentment: accepting your situation to the point that you feel satisfied

and find pleasure in it; no complaints, only thanks!

the way God made her and viewed her. I was frustrated, and I wished I could get into her head to unscramble the twisted thinking in her brain so she could see the truth.

This is the email I received from her two months after our conversation.

Hey, Andrea, how have you been? I don't know if you remember me or not, but we talked for a while in the airport on the way home from Ecuador. We talked about plastic surgery and the fact that I was completely unhappy with everything about my appearance. I just wanted to thank you for talking with me—I must have sounded like a crazy person. Since I've been home, your words have stuck with me. I started searching the Bible for things that God says about me. And you know what? I found out that God made me just the way I am for a reason. I don't need to change anything about me, because he thinks I'm beautiful! Back when we talked, one of the things that I hated most about my appearance was my smile. I thought it was way too big. But now I love it and I smile all the time because I know that my huge smile is just a reflection of the joy I've found in Christ! Anyway, thank you for encouraging me to look into what God says about me instead of focusing on the fact that I don't fit some stupid image. ~ Heather

I didn't know whether to shout, "Sweet!" and give God a high five or shed a few tears. I was truly grateful that Heather had **become** grateful and was now able to thank God for making her as he did.

What about you? Are you open to looking at yourself from a different perspective—from God's perspective? Will you let the Bible, not the teachings of the world we live in, be the truth you live by? Will you choose to make peace with your appearance? Will you choose to be Jesus obsessed and not beauty obsessed?

What? You don't think beauty has a hold on you? Take this quiz and find out!

> **You can learn to love your look and make peace with your appearance.**

# Beauty Obsessed? Take This Quiz!

Circle the number that best describes you.

1. You love wearing Pink Pearl lip gloss but notice the model in the new Cover Girl ad is sporting Rush Red! You switch right away!

| 5 | 4 | 3 | 2 | 1 |
|---|---|---|---|---|
| You bet! | | Yeah, maybe. | | Nope. I'm a pink girl! |

2. A girl in your English class dropped fifteen pounds, and in the last month she's had three dates! You start feeling pudgy and decide to skip lunch.

| 5 | 4 | 3 | 2 | 1 |
|---|---|---|---|---|
| Lunch and dinner! | | Felt fat but ate. | | Happy as I am! |

3. The big red zit that made its appearance in the middle of your chin makes you feel self-conscious all day.

| 5 | 4 | 3 | 2 | 1 |
|---|---|---|---|---|
| Eeks! Of course! | | Sort of but not a big deal. | | No way! |

4. You change your outfit several times almost every day before heading off to school.

| 5 | 4 | 3 | 2 | 1 |
|---|---|---|---|---|
| That's me! | | Well, sometimes. | What goes on stays on! | |

5. You're doing your makeup on the way to school, when you discover your mascara is home in your drawer. You . . .

| 5 | 4 | 3 | 2 | 1 |
|---|---|---|---|---|
| Immediately borrow some! | Feel half dressed. | | | Laugh it off! |

6. You flipped through *CosmoGirl*, noticing every model. After closing the cover, you are . . .

| 5 | 4 | 3 | 2 | 1 |
|---|---|---|---|---|
| Very jealous! | | Slightly depressed. | Glad they looked good! | |

7. It's a bad hair day. Each strand protests the look you're after. You're so frustrated that you end up in tears!

| 5 | 4 | 3 | 2 | 1 |
|---|---|---|---|---|
| Pass the tissue! | | Keep working with it. | | Get real! |

8. On an average morning, it takes you longer than thirty minutes to do your hair and makeup.

| 5 | 4 | 3 | 2 | 1 |
|---|---|---|---|---|
| Always! | | Close but not quite! | | Nope! |

## Scoring

Add up the numbers you circled to find your total score. Then check out this chart.

**29–40 points:** Uh-oh! Obsession alert! You are definitely obsessed! It's time to step back and stop making beauty such a high priority. Put it in perspective by memorizing the Bible verses in this section and stop looking at magazines!

**17–28 points:** On the verge! Ask yourself, "What are some areas in my life where I am overly concerned about my looks?" Pinpoint them. Work with them and embrace them.

**8–16 points:** Beauty balanced! Way to go, girl! You seem to have a healthy perspective on this beauty stuff! Just keep it that way.

# THE GIRL WHO'S GOT IT ALL

You've seen her. She's on the front of *YM* and *Teen People*. She's smiling back at you in a Cover Girl ad. She's sportin' a sassy look in her tight little Bongos or Calvin Kleins. She's the one that makes you think she was born with it; it couldn't just be the Maybelline. She's the one with the perpetually fresh, clean look. You know her, don't you?

She's the picture-perfect chick. The one with the flawless complexion, the pearly whites, the high cheekbones, the shiny hair, the full lips, the long lashes, the right-size nose, the tiny hips, the hint of muscle.

She's the one who can make you stand in front of the mirror thinking, *No way, you've got to be kidding. . . . I can't go anywhere looking like this. . . . I'm too ugly, too fat, too short, too tall, too freckled. . . . Oh, God, couldn't you have done a better job than this?*

She has incredible power, or at least many females allow her to have it. She can make you feel inadequate. Below par. Substandard. Gross. She can get you to try every new product that comes out on the market in hopes of looking more like her. She can keep you from showing up at a friend's birthday party or that concert you didn't want to miss or the cool youth group event you even helped plan. Such power. Such perfection. Such a problem!

Problem?

Yep.

The problem is that this girl who appears to have it all barely even exists!

No one has it all. No one can live up to the unrealistic beauty standard the world sets, that image many try desperately to attain.

# DIGITAL'S WONDERFUL WORLD OF MAGIC

Yeah, a real girl probably posed for the original photo, but that's about where it stops. From there the picture gets scanned onto a computer screen where it's pulled into a program like Photoshop, and then pixel by pixel it's electronically retouched, redesigned, re-created to appear to look . . . perfect. Are you going to believe everything you see? I hope not, because much of it isn't the real deal.

Don't be naïve. Photo editors can change absolutely anything about a photo.

The shape of eyes, lips, and even hips! Nothing is too tough for digital's wonderful world of magic.

Besides changing anything they want, photo editors can also take one person's head and place it on someone else's body. Really. It's been done. (And it's further proof that no one person has it all.) It's even been done to Jennifer Aniston. Yeah, I know you thought this Emmy Award–winning star was nearly perfect and it would be close to impossible for her to appear otherwise, but it happened. In June 2003 Jennifer graced the cover of *Redbook* magazine with a head that was just a little bit too large for its body. Most of us who saw it had to stare at it awhile to figure out exactly why it looked so odd, but sure enough, it was her head! Apparently, there was never a photo shoot. The magazine editors took the liberty of splicing together several different pictures of Jen to make it look as if there had been a live photo session. Rumor has it that a very upset Aniston said that her head, her body, and her arms were from separate pictures. Obviously, she was displeased about appearing with an oversize head. Not exactly the look she usually goes for.

I had a bit of firsthand experience with this retouching stuff during my New York modeling stint. I remember the Saturday morning I woke up with a huge zit. I mean it was a Pike's Peak pimple! I thought it was going to ruin me, just sweep my career right under the rug. See, I was scheduled for a photo shoot for a sports catalog at 8:00 a.m. It was one of my first jobs as a bona fide Wilhelmina girl. But how could I go lugging along my pimple?

I panicked.

I freaked.

I didn't know what to do! The agency was closed because it was the weekend, so I couldn't send an S.O.S. their way. After several laps around the tiny living room in my studio apartment (don't believe that models live in the lap of luxury), I decided I'd better call the photographer to let him know I had to cancel.

That was a tough call. Not only was I feeling paranoid and embarrassed about the whole thing, but as I explained my dreadful plight, this photographer actually had the nerve to start laughing. I didn't see the humor in the situation. Finally the guy said, "Don't you know that we can remove something as simple as a zit from the final photo?" Okay, I really looked like a rookie, because no, I didn't know that!

The truth is, it's done all the time. It's normal. Just a part of the business. But wait. Why does something that's become so normal still threaten to make us look in the mirror and end up feeling discontent with what God has given us? Perhaps because we so easily forget that what we see in magazines is not reality. You and I need to train our mind's eye to recognize the retouched or re-created areas of covers and cosmetic ads.

Hear me on this one, my friend. If looking at models' and actresses' retouched photos ends up making you feel bad about yourself, **shut the magazine!** If seeing skinny, overly made-up chicks on TV or the movies is stirring up rotten thoughts about yourself, **turn off the television!** Yep, hit the power button. It takes guts. Self-discipline always requires inner strength. But ask the Lord, and he will supply you with the fruit of self-control. Obsessing over those doctored-up photos isn't worth beating up your self-esteem (how you feel about yourself).

Now look in the mirror. No, I mean go nose to nose with your reflection. Do you see pores? Do you see blackheads? Do you see tiny facial hairs? Do you see lashes of varying length? Do you see small veins or fading scars?

**Of course you do.**

Now look at that published photo. Do you see the same detail on the model's face? Not likely. So there you have it. Proof of the digital magic wand.

# NOW YOU SEE IT, NOW YOU DON'T

What's really entertaining (especially if you choose to see the folly in all of this) is when you put several photos of the same model or actress side by side. They're never exactly the same. I've seen Sarah Michelle Gellar with undefined biceps, and I've seen her with sculpted muscles. I've seen Angelina Jolie with four different hair colors all in the same week. I've seen Oprah Winfrey with a wide nose and with a narrow nose. I've seen pictures of Cindy Crawford with and without her famous mole. And on it goes!

Fascinating. It's like playing a high-tech game of Now You See It, Now You Don't. At The B.A.B.E. Seminar™ I show two photos of the same model. In both photos she's in a similar pose with her blond hair cascading down one shoulder. She also has her shirt unbuttoned, and she's braless. These, my friend, are what I refer to as "Andrea no-no's"! B.A.B.E.s wear a bra! And it's a really good idea to button your shirt! However, in the case of the exposed model, exhibits one and two of the braless beauty with the open shirt actually help prove my point. In the first photo that flashes up on the screen, the model is fairly flat chested. No, I can't even say that. In photo one there are no signs of breasts—at all! And then photo two appears on the screen. Abracadabra! Full-blown breasts! Incredible. Assuming that blondie isn't packing detachable boobies, there's only one other assumption. What we are seeing is **computer-created cleavage!**

So often the colossal cleavage you see (and sometimes envy) is constructed pixel by pixel by simply adding various shades of brown in just the right areas. This creates a look of round-

FYI: Being the very creative guy he is, God has created tons of different body shapes and sizes, but generally speaking, there are three main frames or bone structures: endomorph (large boned), mesomorph (medium boned), and ectomorph (small boned). Just thought you'd like to know.

ness and depth. The concept is taught in Art 101. To make an object appear 3-D and to give it a sense of roundness, you simply shadow it from light to dark. So in the photo you can see that the front and center of the breasts are light. Then the brown tones begin and become subtly darker as they near the breastbone. Then—this is the best—the very center, the valley of the booming boobies, is light again.

What? How does **that** happen? In real life, it doesn't. In the pictures, it's just another phase of the high-tech phenomena.

Just to be fair, let me say that there are a few models, actresses, and even teen girls who are naturally well endowed. No retouching. No plastic surgery. But most of the skinny bodies with large bosoms we see in print or bouncing down the red carpet are not God-given. Rarely does God put big breasts on a small-boned body! Not impossible but improbable!

## The Perfect Body

The perfect body is tall. It is lean. It is a combination of firmness and fat. It has moles and large knuckles. It has stubborn hair that won't hold a curl.

The perfect body is soft. It is curvy. It is speckled with freckles. It has a nose that is wide. It has pale lips. Its second toe is longer than the first.

The perfect body is large boned. It is strong. It has oily skin and many blackheads. It has slim ankles that wear heels well. It has a rounded stomach.

The perfect body has small breasts. It has dry skin and few blemishes. It has delicate fingers with nails that rarely break. It has full hips.

The perfect body is the one you are in right now; it is a gift from God. It is yours to use as you fulfill God's purposes for you in this life. It is a temple, a sanctuary where the Spirit of its Maker dwells. It is a tent, a temporary home that will pass away. But your soul, your spirit, is the real you. It will last for all of eternity. It is forever.

**That's** perfect.

# FLAWED OR FLAWLESS

The other problem with the phony magazine covers and pre-pampered advertisements is that they can cause us to compare. We've already established the fact that these images are not real, yet being human, we still tend to look at them and then look at ourselves.

Comparing is sorta normal.

Comparing is sorta the thing.

Comparing is sorta stupid. It's unwise.

When they measure themselves by themselves and compare themselves with themselves, they are not wise.

2 Corinthians 10:12 NIV

We will not compare ourselves with each other as if one of us were better and another worse. We have far more interesting things to do with our lives. Each of us is an original.

Galatians 5:26 Message

Comparing can lead to conceit. It feels good at first when you are accumulating accolades and attagirls, when you are patting yourself on the back. But it can lead to a snotty, downward-looking attitude toward others. It clouds your heart! It makes you preoccupied with yourself. It can keep you feeling superior to others but eventually leaves you isolated and alone as your circle of friends becomes smaller and smaller. It's not pretty. Conceit is like pride. It doesn't wear well on Christians. It won't look good on you. It might even trip you up.

Pride goes before destruction,
a haughty spirit before a fall.

Proverbs 16:18 NIV

Don't push your way to the front; don't sweet-talk your way to the top. Put yourself aside, and help others get ahead. Don't be obsessed with getting your own advantage.

Forget yourselves long enough to lend a helping hand.

Philippians 2:3 Message

For everyone who exalts himself will be humbled, and he who humbles himself will be exalted.

Luke 14:11 NIV

On the flip side, comparing can lead to contempt for yourself. It can crush your self-image. It will take your happy attitude about your good hair day or your geometry grade and throw it in the trash when you see that the girl next to you got a higher score or that her hair looks way cuter than yours. It can keep you feeling inferior, making you shy away from opportunities, silencing you when you're called upon, stealing God's plan for you to be all he has called you to be.

Comparing. It keeps you from loving others or loving yourself.

It's not worth it.

Comparing, whether it's to models and actresses or classmates and cousins, may lead to yet another inaccurate conclusion.

**Flaws!**

See, you'll notice that your lips, your nose, your hands, your hips aren't exactly like anyone else's. They don't look like the doctored-up photos that have been made to fit the unrealistic beauty standard.

You may decide you like the photos better. You may decide you have **flaws**.

Or someone else may suggest that you do. Who needs friends like that? Who needs magazine articles that talk about hiding your flaws or camouflaging your imperfections? (Never in *Brio*, of course.) Ever walked past a cosmetic counter and heard a salesperson trying to convince some trusting yet deflated-looking woman seated in her makeover chair that if she just used their brand of foundation or their specially formulated eyeliner, it would correct her flawed complexion or her too-round eyes? Oh yes, her tips and tricks can make thin lips appear fuller and full lips look thinner. And that's just the beginning of what she can do to help minimize or even eliminate "flaws."

**Flaws?**

I detest the word.

Are you going to believe that the same God who created the heavens and the earth, the majestic mountains and the awesome blue ocean, the fragrant flowers and the fabulous fruit trees, didn't have the **ability** to create you without a flaw?

Chew on that a second or two.

You do *not* have flaws. You do *not* have defects. You do *not* have mistakes.

You *do* have one-of-a-kind features that give you a look all your own. You do have unique details! They're given to you by the Master Artist. What are yours? List them here:

I'll share some of mine. It doesn't scare me. In fact, I've grown to love my unique details. Here goes. I have an indent between my nostrils on the under part of my nose. My eyebrows are arched differently. I have a widow's peak, and my hairline is wavy. I have a dark mole on my left cheek. My ears are small. My shoulders are uneven. But my lips are wonderfully even. I love my lips!

**Unique details.** Designed just for you.

They make you special (not freaky or odd). They make you beautiful in a way no one else can be. Truly, there is no one else exactly like you. And truly, aren't you glad? Jot down what you like best about being unique:

# In Their Own Words . . .

I smile every time I think about God, the All-Powerful, creating me. I want to laugh and dance with joy and at the same time cry and bow in awe of him and his love for me.

~ Andrea

I'm constantly humbled when I'm reminded that my heart and attitudes are so much more important and need more work than my appearance.

~ Kelly

God made me the way I am for a reason, and someone somewhere is going to fall in love with me just the way I am.

~ Angela

## When I Look in the Mirror:
# THE NATALIE LLOYD STORY

I've always thought Natalie Lloyd radiates beauty. Natalie couldn't see that beauty without a struggle. Here's her story in her own words:

My mom bought me a "real" crown for one of my elementary school costume parties. I got a lot of use out of that thing! What little girl doesn't want a crown? I would put on my princess costume, wear my crown, and look in my mirror, pretending to be Snow White.

What didn't occur to me, until some kids in my class pointed it out, was that Snow White wasn't in a wheelchair. She didn't have long scars on her legs. She didn't have freckles on her face. She didn't have anything I had.

I can remember riding in the car on the way to church. My dad would look in the rearview mirror and say, "I have the prettiest little girl in the world." My parents told me I was beautiful so much that I almost believed it. Almost. Until I went to school and found so many people determined to point out what I saw as my imperfections. One day when I wore shorts, a little girl a few seats down stared at the scar on my leg (I have one that traces all the way from my hip to my knee on each leg).

"What happened to you?" she said loudly.

My parents had taught me to be proud of the scars on my body—to just answer questions, because most people didn't know what caused them and didn't know how to ask without sounding crazy. So I told her. I was born with a disability called brittle bone disease. I've had several surgeries to repair my femur bone. My scars make me special. She stared at them for a minute and then walked off.

I never wanted to wear shorts again.

Later on the "baby fat," as my mom called it, became a hot topic of discussion. People would make little comments about my body that absolutely broke my heart. Or they would say, "She has such a pretty face." Anyone who has ever had a weight struggle will tell you how much those words can hurt. While someone may be giving a sincere compliment, when the words compute in our minds, they sound more like, "Too bad she isn't skinny or she might be pretty." So as a chubby little girl with big glasses, scars on my legs, a gap between my teeth, and funky hair, I came to a realization: I would never be beautiful. I would simply have to gracefully bow out of anything in my life that would require beauty. I would always be Natalie—the sweet, smart girl. Never the pretty girl. Instead of a princess in my mirror, I looked and saw a twisted mess of scars, broken bones, and freckles.

I stared at myself, murmured, "You are so ugly," and put my plastic crown in the closet. I knew there would never be a crown for this head.

What most girls don't realize during the misery known as junior high is that plenty of changes take place. When I started high school, I was walking (despite the slight limp). I got rid of the baby chub. I waxed my caterpillar eyebrows. My teeth no longer have a space. I highlighted my hair, learned how to dress for my body, and started wearing makeup (which I would never in a million years use to hide my freckles now!).

"Natalie, you're so pretty!" one of my friends said once. I thought I had arrived! I was finally the pretty girl! But when I looked in the mirror, I simply looked for something else about myself to change. I would stare at myself and think,

*You would be prettier if you did something else with your hair.*

*If you had a new outfit.*

*If you looked like her.*

*If you were going out with him.*

*If you joined this club.*

*If you lost just a little more weight . . .*

Despite the receipts I had from stores, the time I spent on my appearance, and the bona fide effort I made to socialize, I was still very insecure. No matter what I did, the girl in the mirror was the same insecure girl she had always been.

One day I was humming the Nicole Nordeman song "Legacy" while I put on my makeup, and a weird thought came to me. When I die I don't want people to say, "Aw, she had such a pretty face." If that's the only legacy I leave, I won't be doing what God wants me to do on this earth. I could picture myself standing before him trying to justify all the time I spent staring in a mirror wishing for a better body instead of reaching out to people all around me who were hurting.

"Can't you see," I could almost hear him saying, "that you'll never find what you're looking for in what other people tell you?

"Can't you see that what's really beautiful in you is me?

"Dye your hair. Fix your teeth. Lose weight. I loved you just as much before as I do now. When you look in the mirror, you see a very blurry picture of what I see when I look into your heart."

That moment I realized that while everywhere I look and everything I see might be concerned with physical appearance, God's opinion is the only opinion that truly matters. And he doesn't think I'm pretty—he thinks I'm beautiful. I'm learning that my confidence doesn't have to be in my appearance, who I'm dating, or how much I do. My confidence doesn't even have to be in me, but it absolutely has to be in him.

I would love to be able to say I've got it all figured out, that I always draw confidence from him and not from myself. But there are still days when I struggle with the body I'm in, mostly because I take my eyes off him and focus on my least favorite features—completely unaware of how wonderfully he works in my weaknesses.

The world says, "You'll only be beautiful if . . ."

God says, "The King is enthralled with your beauty."

Just as we are.

I'm trading a world of plastic crowns and fairy tales for a love that lasts eternally—for a King who dreamed me into being, who loves everything about me, who died just to be with me. What I see in the mirror is only half the story, only what other people first notice. When God looks into my heart, I want his Son's reflection to shine back.

*That* is beautiful.*

* Natalie Lloyd is the author of *Want More? Life* and *Paperdoll*. She is a contributing writer for *SUSIE Magazine* and has the sweetest Southern accent ever!

# EXTREME MAKEOVER

Loving your look is vital. Accepting the Master's design is key. It will put you over the top, way above those who are caught in the appearance pit, those who will do anything to change their features.

Jamie had a very distinguished look. Her jet black hair in contrast with her creamy, pale complexion made her striking. The best part, though, was her laugh. She had a full, fun laugh that communicated the joy and beauty in her heart.

Jamie was a talented artist. Her creativity was unique, because she could see and feel her art. She could also see and feel a part of her that she had grown to almost despise.

Her nose. Her "humpback," as she called it, was the opposite of the petite, straight nose she desired. Jamie focused on her hump-shaped facial centerpiece. Her obsession caused her to fixate on the physical feature, barely seeing all of her true beauty.

Unable to stop the disgust growing inside of her, Jamie turned to a cosmetic surgeon. She signed on the dotted line and underwent rhinoplasty (better known as a nose job).

Did she look better?

Well, she looked different from the original design.

Think about it. Corrective surgery. Even the term implies that what one has is incorrect, that a person's features are wrong!

Plastic surgery. This is a good one too. Plastic. Fake. Not the real thing.

Our society is fanatical about what is considered "that perfect look." They're infatuated with certain features. They believe some doc can wave a wand and create instant beauty. So much so that the idea of taking a person and remaking her has become a national fascination. Which, of course, leads to a national TV show.

*Extreme Makeover. The Swan. Ambush Makeover. Nip and Tuck.*

There will be more of these reality-crazed TV shows in the future.

Thousands and thousands of females have applied to appear on these prime-time productions, to subject themselves to the knife in hopes of getting what they think will finally make them beautiful.

Liposuction. Tummy tuck. Breast implants. Porcelain teeth. Nose reduction.

Chin implant. Brow lift. LASIK eye surgery. Nips and tucks almost everywhere!

Radical redos are done even in the face of potentially serious health consequences such as infection, blood loss, clots, and possible death. Dr. Nikolas Chugay, a Beverly Hills plastic surgeon, says, "The concept of extreme plastic surgery adds land-mines that one must tread lightly on or they can adversely affect the end result and the patient's health." Dr. Chugay also believes that the pre-sentation of reality television plastic surgery is "doctored" in the interest of ratings.* What we don't see on TV is the pain, bruising, oozing, swelling, and depression that hits. This is no small thing!

And what about possible bank-ruptcy?

Big bucks are dished out for these procedures.

US magazine recently reported that the average liposuction goes for about ten thousand dollars for ten pounds of fat. That tiny little nose can be had for about eight thousand bucks.

The world was awestruck with Demi Moore's revamped body when it was debuted in *Charlie's Angels: Full Throttle*. Internet Movie Da-tabase reported that Demi spent a whopping four hundred thousand dollars to get her new look. Let's see . . . that was liposuction to suck fat out of her stomach, buttocks, and thighs; breast implants; Botox injec-tions; collagen injections in her lips; porcelain veneers to whiten her teeth; and skin treatments. Then she hired a nutritionist, a personal trainer, and a kickboxing coach to help her shape up what was left!

Demi is just one of tons of enter-tainers who have changed their origi-nal design. According to US maga-zine, Britney Spears and Christina Aguilera have had breast boosters, while Drew Barrymore has had her breasts reduced. Tori Spelling has un-dergone rhinoplasty. Ah, yes. Just the tip of the iceberg for the stars.

* Dr. Chugay's comments can be found in Lucy Ferreira's article "Is There Extreme Danger Associated with Extreme Makeovers?" (published by KMR Communications).

Of course, no matter how much a person changes her unique details on the outside, she is still the same person on the inside. That part of her needs to be in tip-top shape and looking fine far more than the outside does. And she can't pay a surgeon to make her a decent person who genuinely cares for others. Kindness injec-tions and honesty implants are not yet on the market, nor will they be.

> Thou art worthy, O Lord, to receive glory and honour and power: for thou hast created all things, and for thy pleasure they are and were created.
>
> Revelation 4:11 KJV

## STAMP OF APPROVAL

Will everyone you meet appreciate your unique beauty? Will they immediately recognize the Master's **signature touch** on you?

Probably not.

You might get teased, dissed, or picked on about your appearance. I'll never forget when two guys at school came up to me in class and said, "Hey, we thought you were gonna be a woman. How come you're growing a mustache?" My heart hit the floor. I wished at that moment that I was quick-witted, able to strike back with, "Oh, hey, don't worry. When you grow up maybe you'll have one too." I've never been great with zingers.

You might get called names. A teen girl recently emailed me about the horrible way she felt because a clique of girls were calling her Go-rilla Girl because of her hairy arms. Unfair.

You might get slammed by someone who thinks the world revolves around her and her alone.

How are you going to react to that? You have the power to decide to let the rude comments and uncalled-for actions penetrate your soul or to let them pour off your back.

> Above all else, guard your heart, for it affects everything you do.
>
> Proverbs 4:23 NLT

That's a command. It's not a suggestion. It's given for your protection. If you let everything others say about you seep into your soul and become part of you, you won't like the results. What will you choose to believe about yourself? It matters.

> As he thinks within himself, so is he.
>
> Proverbs 23:7 NASB

Guard your heart, B.A.B.E.!

> I have heard your prayer and seen your tears; I will heal you.
>
> 2 Kings 20:5 NIV

> The LORD is close to the brokenhearted
> and saves those who are crushed in spirit.
>
> Psalm 34:18 NIV

Okay, so that babe-a-licious boy you're crushin' on or the troop of chicas you've been trying to click with may not appreciate your beauty.

But so what? You've still got the look!

What look is that?

The breathtaking beautiful look God intended just for you.

In fact, **God himself placed his stamp of approval on you**!

Rest assured that this stamp is unlike any other. It's not just any ol' stamp. This is not like one of the stickers you find when you open up those undies that come in a nifty three pack. Nor the dot that's stuck on your new T-shirt or socks.

You know. That little green or yellow sticker that proudly proclaims, "Inspected by #61."

Ooh. It always feels a little unsettling to know that #61 has inspected your newly acquired personal items! Nonetheless, they've passed the basic inspection, the basic once-over.

But **you**. Oh, no. Your stamp of approval from God isn't like that at all. You don't get a silly sticker. You don't get a quick examination.

You get the very thumbprint of God himself. He leaves his very own signature on you. That's his seal of approval.

> **No matter how much a person changes her look on the outside, she is still the same person on the inside.**

And you're not scrutinized for perfection. You're rejoiced over with singing.

> The Lord your God is with you,
> he is mighty to save.
> He will take great delight in you,
> he will quiet you with his love,
> he will rejoice over you with singing.
>
> Zephaniah 3:17 NIV

Picture it.

Like the proud Father he is, God steps back to look at you, and he says, **"She's fine! She's divine!"**

Doesn't that send tingles down to your toes? Doesn't that sorta make you wanna shout? Kick up your heels and shout! Stomp your feet, now, and shout! Clap your hands, now, and . . . shout!

Wait, there's more. (I heard you gasp, thinking, *How can there be?* Well, he's God! His love and surprises never end!)

Get ready; here it is:

God sees each of us as totally and **equally** gorgeous! Equally! Yes, our society has a beauty rating system, but God doesn't. He doesn't just hang around up there in heaven scoring us on our looks. There are no zeros and no tens! We're **all** beautiful B.A.B.E.s.

So go ahead.

Celebrate! Celebrate your **thumbprint** of approval. Celebrate your unique details. Celebrate that your Creator and Maker rejoices over you. Celebrate!

## Inside Edition:
## Behind the Scenes with Professional Model
# Laura Krauss Calenberg

If Laura Krauss Calenberg had known then what she knows now, she wouldn't have moved to New York City at eighteen with her life savings in her pocket. But this Indiana girl had modeling on her mind.

Pounding the pavement, knocking on doors, running out of cash, fighting those who tried to take advantage of her naïveté, turning down topless dancing jobs, turning to waitressing, Laura hung in there and eventually moved to Paris. That's where she got her real start. She found herself strutting down the runway for top designers like Christian Dior, Armani, Chanel, Lanvin, and Yves Saint Laurent. She also appeared on the covers of the hottest magazines.

Currently with the Ford Modeling Agency, Laura is best known in the industry for her long legs. You'll find them in ads for pantyhose and the like. And those incredibly long (and very insured) legs still land her modeling jobs, even after she gave birth to two kids. Though she still models professionally, her real passion these days is modeling Christ.

Laura says living with one foot in the Bible and one foot in the world doesn't work. There's no peace. Laura recalls, "I was constantly searching not only for how far I would go but for who I was and what I believed in. I saw what some of the other models worshiped, and it scared me. Finally I had to ask myself and decide, *Am I going to serve myself and get ahead, or am I serving someone much higher?* I chose Christ."

A difficult thing to do in the beauty and fashion industry? Definitely. Rarely does a committed Christian make it to supermodel status. Why? Because those in the power positions may cut you off for not doing what they want. Yes, there are some people in high positions who are understanding. If you are working and doing a great job, some will honor your convictions. But you may not make as much money, because you have opted out of doing certain jobs. Laura has chosen not to model for those lucrative alcohol, cigarette, and lingerie ads. Compromising isn't an option for those who really desire to glorify God with their lives. No Victoria's Secret layouts, *Sports Illustrated* swimsuit editions, Abercrombie & Fitch, and so on!

Today Laura spends most of her time discipling new Christians through the ministry she and her husband of seventeen years, Jeff Calenberg, started called Models for Christ (www.modelsforchrist .com). They offer God's light in the darkness of the modeling and fashion industry. Bible studies, witnessing, outreach projects, and hands-on service projects are what they are all about. They help feed the homeless in the city and organize clothing drives for the needy.

Is it more fulfilling than a photo shoot?

Way more.

Laura says, "Some of the most beautiful women in the world are the most insecure women I've ever met. There's a lot of rejection in this business, and it's easy to start feeling you're not pretty enough or thin enough. One thing God has taught me is that true beauty is on the inside."

The business breeds insecurity. If you're not getting the hottest jobs and keeping your face on covers, the industry forgets about you.

The Bible breeds security. You are never forgotten.

Modeling for the industry won't fill the empty void we all feel on the inside.

Modeling for Christ will.

Inner attractiveness is what it's all about.

What has God taught Laura about true beauty? "I can have my outside package looking good, but if I'm not being like Christ on the inside, it's ugly. We can be ugly at the drop of a hat." Yep, being Christlike is beautiful.

Want to know Laura's advice to teens wanting to get into modeling? "I don't encourage girls to get into the business," she says, "though I help those who are already in it to get them the right information. In fact, 80 percent of the girls I consult, I tell them not to pursue it. It takes a strong faith, a strong personality, and a strong network of support."

Many girls think they are strong, and then they get eaten up. Never should a girl get into modeling unless she and her parents know beyond a shadow of a doubt that it's a God thing. Only then can you rely on God's protection and his favor to open the right doors at the right time. But his agenda will never be for a girl to just be a supermodel. His purpose would be to use her in the industry to represent him and to lead others to him, to defend the faith using the Bible. Can you do that? Laura can and does.

You want to be a model?

No problem.

Model Christ!*

* On my next trip to NYC, Laura and I plan to order up some café mochas and chat up our modeling stories. Go to www.modelsforchrist .com to nab the details on Laura's mission to the fashion industry.

# redefining Beautiful

Raise your hand if you'd like a fresh perspective on this beauty stuff. That's great, because here it comes! (You can put your hand down now.)

A camera is an important tool for an artist. As an artist in training (I love to oil paint), I found the need to own a camera that allowed me to focus on an object I might like to paint. If I put the setting on auto focus, the camera decides what will be clearly seen and what will not. I don't choose.

However, if I switch to manual focus, I control the settings and what I choose to focus on. For instance, my girlfriend and I went on a three-day whirlwind trip from where I live in central California, over to the coast, down through the Danish community of Solvang, over the mountains, and back to my house. At one time we decided to take a road less traveled (literally) that wound through the mountains. It was so steep I dared not look down. But it was also gorgeous. Soon I noticed the most vivid purple flowers (I adore purple), and my fear was replaced with the desire to capture the scene on film. On auto focus, the camera put the flowers in focus. Great. But on manual, I then focused on the middle scene, the mountains, and then on the distant scene, the ocean. So cool. I was not limited to zeroing in on what the camera selected—the object closest to me and most obvious. I got a different picture, a new perspective, by choosing to **focus** on something else.

We can get a fresh perspective on beauty by switching from auto focus to manual focus. We can choose to put our attention elsewhere. It's time to focus on something other than the number on the scale, the size of our new jeans, and the covers of the magazines. We need a more accurate definition. A more divine definition. Check it out:

> But the LORD said to Samuel, "Do not look at his appearance or at the height of his stature . . . for God sees not as man sees, for man looks at the outward appearance, but the LORD looks at the heart.
>
> 1 Samuel 16:7 NASB

Don't be concerned about the outward beauty that depends on jewelry, or beautiful clothes, or hair arrangement. Be beautiful inside, in your hearts, with the lasting charm of a gentle and quiet spirit which is so precious to God.

1 Peter 3:3–4 TLB

Do you see the key word in these verses? Okay, check again. I'll wait.

It starts with *h* and ends with *t*.

**Heart.**

See, real beauty from God's perspective isn't about your hips or your hairdo; it's about your heart. It's not about being zit free or fat free; it's about being jealousy free, grudge free, anger free, and selfishness free. It's all about the inside. All about your heart.

That's how God defines beauty.

## God-Beauty

Truly beautiful young women aren't those who grace the covers of *Elle Girl* or *Seventeen*. They're the ones who are kind, patient, caring, and compassionate. They're the ones who make you feel special, like you matter. They're the ones who unselfishly think of others first; they're faithful friends; they're honest—choosing not to cheat, lie, or gossip; they're morally good. **Pure hearted**. Willing to do what is right even if they get slammed for it. They're the ones who want to honor God with their lives. That's God-Beauty!

B.A.B.E.s with God-Beauty smile at those who are mean to them. They respect their parents and teachers. They include those less popular. They ask, "What would Jesus do?" and they do it to the best of their ability. They glow from the inside out. (Do **you** glow, girl?)

So how does a girl get God-Beauty?

### By making her heart Christ's home

"And I pray that Christ will be more and more at home in your **hearts** as you trust in him." ~ Ephesians 3:17 NLT

**Being beautiful isn't about looking good.**

## By putting God first in her life

"'Of all the commandments, which is the most important?' 'The most important one,' answered Jesus, 'is this: . . . Love the Lord your God with all your **heart** and with all your soul and with all your mind and with all your strength.'" ~ Mark 12:28–30 NIV

## By allowing God to spotlight major areas in her heart that need changing

"Search me, O God, and know my **heart**; test me and know my thoughts. Point out anything in me that offends you, and lead me along the path of everlasting life." ~ Psalm 139:23–24 NLT

## By focusing her thoughts, motivations, and purposes on God

"Let the words of my mouth and the meditation of my **heart** be acceptable in Your sight, O LORD, my rock and my Redeemer." ~ Psalm 19:14 NASB

## By studying the Bible, allowing it to live in her, and allowing it to purify her

"For the word of God is living and active and sharper than any two-edged sword, and piercing as far as the division of soul and spirit, of both joints and marrow, and able to judge the thoughts and intentions of the **heart**." ~ Hebrews 4:12 NASB

"Create in me a clean **heart**, O God. Renew a right spirit within me." ~ Psalm 51:10 NLT

## By trusting God

"Do not let your **hearts** be troubled. Trust in God; trust also in me." ~ John 14:1 NIV

## By beholding the Lord

"One thing I ask of the LORD, this is what I seek: that I may dwell in the house of the LORD all the days of my life, to gaze upon the **beauty** of the LORD and to seek him in his temple." ~ Psalm 27:4 NIV

**Real beauty from God's perspective isn't about your hips or your hairdo; it's about your heart!**

Is it possible for you to have God-Beauty? Is it possible for you to possess a beautiful heart that is home to Christ, that puts God first, that is willing to be changed by God and the Bible, that is clean and pure, that trusts God, and that beholds the Lord, looking at his beauty and making it your own? Is that possible?

**Absolutely.**

Why not get started right now? Answer the following questions, and you'll be on your way!

- Is Jesus Christ living in my heart?

    _____ yes   _____ no   _____ not sure

    If you answered "no" or "not sure," turn immediately to pages 115–116. That's right. Go straight there. Come back when you're done.

- Is God first in my life?

    _____ yes   _____ no   _____ probably not, but I want to change!

    If you're serious about putting God first, then it's time for a prayer powwow! Ask the Father to show you the areas of your life where you're putting him in that number 2, 3, or 4 spot (too much time in sports, dishonoring your parents, filling your brain with thoughts of a hot boy from biology class, not tithing, skipping church, etc.). Jot them here:

    Now do some brainstorming to come up with a few changes you can make so that God is in the prime spot (have daily time with him, participate in fewer activities, get involved in youth group, check yourself on your music, etc.). Jot them here:

- Are there areas in my life that I know are offending God? Are there things I am doing that I know are wrong? Confess these to him right now.

**True repentance requires a change of direction.** What is your plan for putting the brakes on these activities and then doing a U-turn to go God's direction? This might be hard. You might have to end a relationship, get some new friends, and spend some Saturday nights home with Mom or Dad instead of at an unsupervised party. But the load off your heart will be worth it. Be a brave B.A.B.E. Write your changes here:

- What are the meditations of my heart? What do I dwell on, spend time thinking about?

  What kind of things does God want me to be thinking about? (Hint: Read Philippians 4:8–9.) List them:

- Do I read the Bible and allow it to purify me by obeying it?
  _____ yes  _____no  _____ sometimes
  Write a brief prayer petitioning God's help:

- Am I trusting God with every area of my life?
  _____ yes  _____ no  _____ not sure
  If not, where do you not trust him? What is keeping you from it? Commit your response to prayer:

- Do I spend time in his presence, beholding his beauty and allowing him to love on me as I love on him?
  _____ yes  _____ no
  If you struggle with this, go take a worship walk. With each few steps, tell God what you are thankful for, meditate on a Bible verse, share your heart with him. He's always there and always listening. He loves the sound of your voice!

You are now on your way to true God-Beauty. Don't let anyone or anything hold you back from being the beautiful you that you were created to be!

# BLIND Beauty:
# The Ginny Owens Story

God has granted to this generation a young songwriter who glows with God-Beauty. Her lyrics possess a heartfelt, personal, and spiritual quality. These are words birthed from a passionate relationship with Jesus, birthed from a heart that has sat at the feet of Jesus and had its fill from his Word. It's a heart that has become beautiful because it reflects the beauty of its Maker.

Her name is Ginny Owens. She is blind—physically.

Ginny began singing about the same time she learned to talk. As a toddler, she started harmonizing to melodies played on the piano. She was a natural.

As a toddler, she also lost her vision. Doctors were unable to save her sight.

Ginny grew up climbing trees, riding bikes, studying hard, attending college, and even teaching music. However, since her employers focused on her blindness, Ginny chose to focus on her songwriting.

I first met Ginny after a concert she did in central California. She was led onto the stage by a gentleman who then accompanied her on drums. As she began to sing, I was instantly taken with the beauty of her voice and her piano abilities. But it's her lyrics that rock my soul. And not only mine. Ginny's first CD, *Without Condition*, was an incredible success and won her the New Artist of the Year at the Dove Awards. The world adored her sophomore project, *Something More*, and *Beautiful* has touched the hearts of people all over the country. Ginny's insightful songwriting ability is obviously founded in an intimate relationship with Jesus.

When I met with Ginny after the concert, I found her to be gracious, witty, and very real. Her transparency was refreshing.

Her beauty isn't about styling gels and eye-shadow colors. It's about having a heart like Jesus. In the song "Call Me Beautiful," Ginny shows the value in getting our stamp of approval from the

Lord. He calls us beautiful! And it's his love that opens our souls and allows us to be ourselves—to sense that we belong, we are valued, we can overcome anything because of the new confidence we feel as we bask in his love. And when are we assured of God's love? When we are with him!

Grab your Bible and read Psalm 27:4. (Yeah, I know you could just flip back a few pages and read it from this book, but really, you gotta see it in the Bible for yourself.) Go ahead. Do it. I'll wait.

Okay, now rewrite it in your own words:


When we dwell in God's presence, we are changed.
When we dwell in God's Word, we are changed.
When we look to his beautiful ways, we are changed.
We become like him.

Take a moment right now and ponder this question. "What keeps me from spending more time in the presence of God and in his Word?" Be honest. Record your response here:


Would you like to see with new eyes? Would you like to have a beauty that transcends physical sight? Would you like to quit focusing so much on the outer you and develop a more beautiful inner you? Would you like to look past people's faces and know them by their hearts? You can do it. Write a prayer asking God to help you, and tell him the steps you plan to take! Pick up that pen again and put your prayer here so you can see it over and over!


Ginny Owens is one incredible woman. She's blind, but she can see. Her heart is so drawn in by the heart of God that her life reflects his beauty. She faithfully uses her gift of songwriting to capture the heart of God, the heart of his Word, and then gives it as a gift to the heart of his people. How beautiful.*

*I met up with Ginny at Station 3:16 in downtown Bakersfield, California—it's only the coolest Christian coffee house and concert hall ever.

# ONE HOT DIVINE DIVA

Kara came to me after attending The B.A.B.E. Event™, put a note in my hand, and turned and walked away. Before I could catch her, she was gone. I slowly opened the neatly folded paper and read,

> Dear Andrea,
>
> I know that God views me as a beautiful creation of his, but I don't feel beautiful. What am I supposed to do with these feelings? How can I change them? I want to *feel* beautiful.
>
> Kara

Ever feel like Kara? Seeing your beauty and appreciating your unique design may be one thing, but feeling lovely and attractive may be a whole other story.

I propose to you that feeling beautiful comes from a heart that possesses and practices God-Beauty. It comes from a **decision** to adjust your thinking and see beauty as God sees it. It's **choosing** to see yourself through God's eyes. Note the bolded words.

But it's more. It's putting feet on your inner loveliness and becoming a **B.A.B.E. in Action**! When you start acting in beautiful ways, you'll start feeling beautiful. When you choose to have a giving heart, a loving heart, a kind heart, and you act on those emotions and character traits, beauty is sure to follow. You'll feel beautiful. And no one can take that feeling away from you.

I think Jesus must have felt beautiful on the inside. That might sound weird in reference to him, but think about it. He was always doing beautiful things from his heart. He had compassion on the hungry and fed the crowds. He raised the widow's only son from the dead. He put a mud-spit mixture on a man's eyes, giving him sight. He wept over Mary and Martha's pain when they lost their brother—he felt their pain even though he had plans to call Lazarus out of the grave. He ate with sinners, talked to outcasts, touched the untouchable lepers, and loved playing with the children. He was, as we should be, kind, gentle, and the goodness of God wrapped in a body!

**Do you want to feel beautiful 24/7?**
**Become a B.A.B.E. in Action!**

His sincere and heartfelt actions produced a stunning beauty. This type of beauty is eternal. It produces a feeling that will last from here to heaven. It's this inside-out beauty that makes you **one hot divine diva**! A blessed beauty on fire with the love of God and sharing it with others. Inside and out, what a **beautiful** you.

# The B.A.B.E. Checklist

Are you finally getting the full picture about what a fabulous beauty you are? Do you understand the difference between God-Beauty and the world's beauty? Let's find out. Read the following statements, then mark your answers. Take note of the ones you can't yet answer with a heartfelt "yes!" Make them a matter of prayer.

**Yes   No   Almost**

____ ____ ____  I believe I am handcrafted by God.

____ ____ ____  I clearly see that our culture has a beauty standard, and it is unfair, unrealistic, and unintended by God.

____ ____ ____  I believe that in God's eyes I have a beauty all my own.

____ ____ ____  I am celebrating my look instead of comparing myself to others.

____ ____ ____  I agree that I do not have flaws or defects in my appearance.

____ ____ ____  I can see that beauty is about more than physical attractiveness.

____ ____ ____  I look at magazine covers and product ads with an analytical attitude, knowing that much of what I see is fake.

____ ____ ____  I understand that my value, my acceptance, my satisfaction, and my success does not come from my appearance.

____ ____ ____  I am learning to let go of hurtful remarks from others and choosing to forgive them.

____ ____ ____  I am ready to start serving others so I can feel real beauty.

____ ____ ____  I am willing to shift my focus away from worldly beauty to total God-Beauty.

____ ____ ____  I understand that developing God-Beauty is up to me.

____ ____ ____  I understand that the inner qualities of my heart are what make me stunningly attractive.

# A IS FOR

# ACCe

PTeD!

# WANTING TO BE WANTED:

## Heidi's Story

I saw a young woman with two short pigtails sitting in front of my husband's desk. Apparently, she was interviewing for the bookkeeping job at our church. I did a double take at the tattoo peeking out from under her sleeveless shirt. Not to sound judgmental, but she didn't look the clerical type. Could she handle the accounting of a big church? Would she run away with the church's money? Would she even show up for work regularly? I was baffled.

Nonetheless, here was this person. And my husband hired her!

As I watched her, this girl named Heidi, I became curious.

What was her deal, her story? I knew she had one.

Indeed. Here it is.

Heidi got pregnant when she was eighteen. Well, the first time, anyway.

See, her dad packed his bags and walked out on her, her two brothers, and her mom when she was only eight. Heidi couldn't understand. Why did he leave them? When did he stop loving them? What had she done wrong?

Feeling rejected by the only important man in her life, Heidi's confused, hurt feelings turned to anger. The courts ordered her and her brothers to spend summers with her dad. But the barriers she had put around her heart to keep out further hurt didn't work too well. Soon after the divorce, her dad introduced her to his new wife and her two daughters, who were now his.

Heidi's inner wounds stung all over again. These two girls would be living with **her** dad. It wasn't fair. It wasn't right. It felt like double rejection.

Unwanted. That's what she concluded.

Eventually she refused to even call him "father." Resentment had set in. But deep down what she longed for was for him to come back home, to say it was all a huge mistake, to ask for her forgiveness, to take her in his arms, to try to win at cards like he used to. She needed **him**, yet he was the one she was angry with.

Heidi's mom did her best. After the divorce she moved herself and her kids across the country to California. She worked full-time but would also work nights when necessary. It was hard to make ends meet. Heidi knew her mom was trying, but she and her brothers were often left on their own.

With hurt in her heart and free time on her hands, Heidi fell in with a group of teens who were smokers and drinkers. Eventually she started using weed and alcohol. Friday nights, Saturday nights, Sunday afternoons—any time was a good time for weed. Or so she thought. At least it put a Band-Aid on the anxiety she felt over her life—all fifteen years of it.

Just for kicks, one night Heidi invited a straight-A, churchgoing friend to a party with her. They both got wasted. The friend got busted. Her dad came to pick her up. No one came for Heidi. That jolted her.

Partying had become her passion, and it was spinning out of control. She was using drugs daily, skipping school, and failing classes. Smart enough to see she was in a downward spiral, Heidi turned to her mom for help. A local rehab center agreed to admit her. After sixty days of agonizing withdrawal, group therapy, and one-on-one counseling, Heidi left clean.

But not cured.

Being high seemed better than facing her reality. She eventually resumed her status as party girl. At least she felt included. Wanted.

Especially by Luke. They had quickly become an item.

Heidi desired arms around her. They seemed to fill an emptiness. Yet she knew his embrace was only a substitute for the one from whom she really needed love and affirmation: her dad. At least that's the love she thought she needed.

Thinking she loved Luke, she didn't stop the passion when she should have. She wanted someone to notice her, to be there for her, unlike her parents. Giving herself to him cut deep, especially after she found he had cheated on her. They broke up.

At seventeen, Heidi got invited to a youth group where she heard about this man named Jesus, who was God's Son, sent to earth to pay the death penalty for the sins of humanity. God

**If you met Heidi today, you would never guess her past. You'd see her heartfelt smile and clear eyes. You'd hear about her college classes, the skateboard ministry she runs, and oh yes, she'd dish all about her fiancé. She has become such a B.A.B.E.!**

loved her enough to send Jesus; Jesus loved her enough to die for her. That was a love she had never experienced. Heidi prayed, asking Jesus to rescue her, wanting to be rid of the sins from her past. She was baptized. She felt warm on the inside.

Yet that feeling didn't last, because she wasn't taken into a Bible study or placed under the wing of a mentor. She never filled her mind with the truth of the Bible, allowing her to be made truly whole. She wasn't tight with the girl who had taken her to the youth group.

She did, however, have a Bible that she had kept with her. It had sat on her bookshelf in every city she'd ever lived in, but the blue leather cover had been unopened, the pretty silver-edged pages untouched.

Back into her carefree charade, Heidi soon found herself involved with a much older guy. It was a short time later that she discovered she was pregnant and scared. The guy said he would support whatever she wanted, then quickly vanished from her life. The ultimate insult. She went to speak to his family, a Christian family, only to hear that the pregnancy was her problem, not theirs. Turning to her family, Heidi was told to get rid of "it" or get out and have the baby on her own. Feeling stuck and alone, she made the appointment at an abortion clinic. Her mom went with her when the day arrived.

Soon after that she left town—hoping to leave the bad memories behind. But she met a guy, fell hard, and moved in with him. Maybe he would be able to fill the emptiness and end the insecurity she was feeling. Maybe he would want her longer than the last guy had. Then again, maybe not.

## In Her Own Words . . .

You will never feel totally accepted until you let God be your all-in-all.

Be picky about what girls you hang with—they *will* influence you.

Dress modestly. It will keep guys from hitting on you.

Parents screw up. Forgive them.

Trust me; there is nothing good in a drink, a joint, or a pill.

Abortion is *never* the answer.

Get into the Bible! It will help you recognize Satan's traps and give you discernment.

Life is full of choices. Each choice has a consequence. Choose wisely.

~ Heidi

Within a year, another pregnancy test proved positive. Her guy wasn't interested in marriage or kids. With no one supporting her, Heidi planned another trip to the abortion clinic. She hated to walk through those clinic doors, walk by the people near the front steps—some begging her not to abort but to give her baby to them, others hurling rude comments and embarrassing remarks.

After two pregnancies and two abortions, Heidi found herself in a funk, fully depressed. She couldn't stomach the fact that she had been "stupid twice," as she describes it. Her heart was broken over her actions, her lifestyle, her existence. She contemplated ending it all.

Instead, from somewhere deep inside, she found herself thinking, *There's got to be more than this*, and she remembered the Bible she owned and the God who said he loved her. She searched out her Bible, cracked open the pages, and began to read. And as she read, a new hope, a new peace, a new life took hold deep within her. And there was something else. A feeling she wasn't used to but the very thing she had been searching for all along. Acceptance.

**The A in B.A.B.E. is for accepted!**

Heidi knew God had the right to come down on her and give her what she truly deserved. He could reject her in total disgust for all she had done. He could use the opportunity to dog her unholy living. He could punish her in some way just to teach her a lesson. He could let her know how worthless she was. And he could refuse to forgive her. He could leave her trapped in her shamefulness and guilt.

But he did none of those things.

Instead, he granted her unearned mercy.

Irreversible forgiveness.

Unlimited grace.

And amazing acceptance.

She called an old party pal who had become a Christian and said, "Take me to church, girl! I'm ready!" Heidi totally got into God, and she discovered that his truth, found in the Bible, could actually fill up the empty, lonely, insecure, anxious, and rejected places in her heart.

First, God started healing the guilt, the shame, and the grief she felt over the abortions. Then she felt God saying, "Give me all of the hurt and disappointments over your dad, and let me love you." His love is like a healing salve. It wasn't like the turn-it-on, turn-it-off kind of love. It was real and unending. It was healing.

Soon God created in Heidi a desire to live a clean and pure life.* She stopped dating altogether, cleaned up

---

* The Bible refers to this as the sanctification process. To be sanctified means to be set apart from the ways of the world as the Holy Spirit trains us to live a life that is obedient and pleasing to God. It's the process of us becoming more and more like Jesus. It's the process of us acting like the children of God that we are.

her foul mouth, and said good-bye to alcohol and drugs—this time without the help of a rehab program.

> "Even if my father and mother abandon me, the LORD will hold me close." ~ Psalm 27:10 NLT

Heidi's desire to change grew as she pursued a personal relationship with Jesus. In fact, she discovered that the acceptance she had longed for from her dad and other men was filled only by her relationship with her heavenly Father. It was the true acceptance, the ultimate acceptance, the one that healed the broken places, sealing each crack with peace and joy.

# Because You're Worth It

What God did for Heidi he does for you and me. Do I really mean to suggest that if you or I had been in Heidi's shoes, he would have treated us the same way? That he would have offered forgiveness, love, and acceptance?

Absolutely.

In fact, he already has about a bazillion times.

And why in heaven's name does he do that? We know our hearts; doesn't he? We know how rotten we can be. We know what we'd like to do to those people who irritate us or get in our way. We know the thoughts we have about our parents. We know how we honestly feel about ourselves at times. We know our weaknesses and how we seek to fulfill them in the wrong ways.

Why would God treat us in ways we don't deserve?

Because he is a pro at looking past our sin and seeing our need to be loved, feel wanted, and be completely accepted. And because in his book **you are worth it!** That, my friend, is called **unconditional acceptance**. It's amazing. It's powerful. It's free.

How would you define unconditional acceptance? Jot it down in your own words:

Now give an example of it:

Have you ever longed for that kind of acceptance? Be honest. We all have at one time or another. Every living, breathing person longs for this unconditional acceptance.

To be accepted means

~ to be received with open arms (like when you go visit your grandma or when the little kids you babysit for run up to hug your legs)

~ to be acknowledged (like when your coach congratulates you for a job well done)

~ to become part of something (like when you made National Honor Society because of those good grades you worked so hard to achieve)

~ to be approved (like when your photography was selected for display)

~ to be given a favorable response (like that smile that spreads across your mom's face when you clean your room and vacuum the house without being asked and without being paid! It's called being in a family!)

Being accepted feels grand, doesn't it? Well, doesn't it? It gives you a **sense of freedom** to be yourself. It gives you a **sense of belonging**. It gives you a **sense of security**. Those are things we all need deep inside.

If you're thinking that you **aren't** sure how it feels because you aren't sure if you have ever been accepted like this, then, girl, you and I have a divine appointment. Right here, right now. You and me. And God (that's where the divine part comes in). There are a few things God wants you to understand about him, his ways, and his Word (the Bible).

Here goes. God is the acceptor. He is the one who, without a shadow of a doubt, has accepted you. We've already established the fact that he has put his stamp of approval on you. He adores your physical appearance. And now, if that isn't enough to make your heart happy, here comes another incredible truth: he accepts you 100 percent! Oh yeah, with all your oddities, quirks, brokenness, sinfulness, moodiness, sassiness, and of course, let's not overlook your winsome personality and loving heart! He takes the good and the not so good! He approves of you as a person, as his child.

Check it out:

> So accept each other just as **Christ has accepted you**.
>
> Romans 15:7 NLT

> But now we have a far better hope, for **Christ makes us acceptable to God**, and now we may draw near to him.
>
> Hebrews 7:19 TLB

See? Accepted!

Never does the Bible say that in order to be accepted by the heavenly Father we need to clean up our acts, stop cheating on tests, obey our parents, quit being flirts, or read our Bibles ten times a day. We do those things out of love and obedience to the Lord, because we are so grateful for his love and acceptance that we want to show it. We want to honor him. But we don't do them to be accepted. See the difference? Don't

overlook the key point from Hebrews 7:19—it's Jesus who makes us 100 percent acceptable to God. How? When? Why? Oh, I love your inquisitive nature! He makes us acceptable when we believe in him and give our lives to him. Did you do that yet? If not, go straight to page 115–116 to learn how!

Okay, God is the one who does the accepting. And because he accepts you, you become the recipient of his unconditional, unequivocal, unending acceptance. You are the acceptee (I'm not sure that's even a word, but you get it, right?). You're the one who is accepted. Okay, maybe not every person you want to have accept you actually will, but, girl, the God of the universe, the Maker of all things visible and invisible, says you are acceptable. The very one who chose to have his only Son die a shameful and excruciating death so you could be free from the penalty of your sin, the one true living God who knows every secret in your heart, absolutely adores you. You are loved! You are accepted.

**If God loved you so much that he sent Jesus to die in your place, then you can love you too!**

# I CHOOSE YOU!

If you thought understanding that you are accepted was too good to be true, you better sit down for this one. You, B.A.B.E., have been **chosen**!

You are not secondhand or thrift-store quality. So untangle any thoughts you might have of being unwanted and set your emotions straight. You are not a Goodwill girl! Yeah, Goodwill is great for finding some slightly used or pretty funky threads, but it's not okay for how you feel about yourself or how you view you! God has chosen you, and I'm going to prove it to you right now. Ready for this? Here goes:

> **I have chosen you** and will not throw you away.
>
> Isaiah 41:9 TLB

> Of all the people on earth, the LORD your **God has chosen you** to be his own special treasure.
>
> Deuteronomy 7:6 NLT

> I have called you friends. . . . You did not choose Me but **I chose you**.
>
> John 15:15–16 NASB

> But you are a **chosen people**, a royal priesthood, a holy nation, a people belonging to God, that you may declare the praises of him who called you out of darkness into his wonderful light.
>
> 1 Peter 2:9 NIV

Chosen. Hand selected. Picked out. Not only should that give you warm fuzzies and cause you to feel like the princess you are, but it can change your life if you let it. And so can the next truth you're going to discover. So don't touch that dial—there's more stuff you gotta know about the real you!

# WHOSE YOU ARE

We all need affirmation. We all want to know the answer to "Did I do well? Am I good? Do I count? Am I lovable? Am I worth it?"

B.A.B.E.! Close your eyes and see me desperately trying to balance on the top of a tall stool with a megaphone to my lips, shouting, **"Ask God! Summon your Maker to see if you matter!"**

See, God doesn't use a flawed human values system that judges us unfairly. He uses a divine system that isn't based on our performance, appearance, athletic abilities, or academic achievements. (Really, God isn't nearly as stressed over your SAT scores as you and your parents may be. He already knows what college you're going to and is wondering why you're so uptight! Trust!)

So if it's not based on what we do, what is it based on, you ask?

**Whose** you are.

And whose are you?

His.

You are his child. Therefore, you are known, included, valued, and loved! Whew.

Lay your eyes on this:

You are **known** by him!

My sheep hear My voice, and **I know them**, and they follow Me.

John 10:27 NASB

O Lord, you have examined my heart and **know everything about me**. You **know** when I sit or stand. When far away you know my every thought. You chart the path ahead of me, and tell me where to stop and rest. Every moment, you **know** where I am. You **know** what I am going to say before I even say it. You both precede and follow me, and place your hand of blessing on my head. This is too glorious, too wonderful to believe! I can never be lost to your Spirit! I can never get away from my God!

Psalm 139:1–7 TLB

You are **included** by him—into his family, the body of Christ!

But now God has placed the members, each one of them, in the body, just as He desired.

1 Corinthians 12:18 NASB

You are of great worth to him—highly **valuable**!

Your inner self, the unfading beauty of a gentle and quiet spirit . . . is of **great worth in God's sight.**

1 Peter 3:4 NIV

Are not two sparrows sold for a penny? Yet not one of them will fall to the ground apart from the will of your Father. And even the very hairs on your head are all numbered. So don't be afraid; **you are worth more than many sparrows.**

Matthew 10:29–31 NIV

You are **loved** by him! And it's a love that sticks like glue, because nothing can separate you from his love.

For God **loved the world** so much that he gave his only Son so that anyone who believes in him shall not perish but have eternal life.

John 3:16 TLB

Do you think anyone is going to be able to **drive a wedge between us and Christ's love for us**? There is no way! Not trouble, not hard times, not hatred, not hunger, not homelessness, not bullying threats, not backstabbing, not even the worst sins listed in Scripture. . . . None of this fazes us because **Jesus loves us**. I'm absolutely convinced that nothing—nothing living or dead, angelic or demonic, today or tomorrow, high or low, thinkable or unthinkable—**absolutely nothing can get between us and God's love** because of the way that Jesus our Master has embraced us.

Romans 8:35–39 Message

Known! Included! Valued! Loved!

All of this. Why? Because you are his. Because you **belong** to him.

# eBaY BUYS

Have you ever done the eBay thing? When I first caught wind of the possibility of selling items over the Internet, I thought it sounded like a huge blast. A new way of shopping. A gigantic cyberspace kind of yard sale. A high-tech way to unload your used goods or to scoop up someone else's unwanted treasures. Like a flea market free-for-all. If you've ever logged on, you know that eBay has been a smashing success. There are antiques, collectables, and great deals of all kinds. Anyone can sign up to sell anything! Even celebrities' pre-owned items or movie props have hit the list. Just for fun, circle the stuff you think would bring in the biggest bucks:

Carly Patterson's gold medal leotard **or** your old tutu?

Your best friend's prom dress **or** Jennifer Aniston's wedding gown?

Laura Bush's personal pen set **or** your mom's favorite BIC?

An autographed picture of Hillary Duff **or** one of Hillary Hansen (who?)?

Miss America's crown **or** Miss Arkadelphia's crown?

No-brainers, right?

You can pretty much guess which items will pull in the money. Why is that? Because some items are considered more valuable because of whom they belong to! Even though your best gal pal is the greatest, to the eBay buyers, her perfectly pretty prom dress would be considered rags next to Jennifer Aniston's wedding gown.

Now, turn your brain on full blast for this one.

Imagine your value since you belong to the Creator of the universe, the one and only God! Your worth is off the charts. **You are priceless.** (Of course, you wouldn't ever be up for sale on eBay.) Priceless. It doesn't get any better than this!

In primitive cultures and in many places still today, brides are "purchased" from their parents with a dowry. A dowry might consist of anything from grain to turkeys to cattle to camels. (Really,

**Can you believe that in some cultures the newlyweds don't work the first year of marriage? They just get to know each other! I like it!**

someone tried to buy a friend of my husband's while on a mission trip and offered three camels! They had to explain she wasn't for sale!) In some countries the average bride might be exchanged for two cows, while a strong, hardy one would go for three. A lesser bride might bring her parents only one cow.

Picture this. A wealthy, handsome, strong young man rides into town looking for a bride. Let's call him Mr. Pitt. The parents in town with eligible daughters primp them up to be paraded for the man. After carefully scrutinizing the selection of maidens, the wealthy young man shocks the village folk by choosing a young woman whom they thought was undesirable. She was quiet, frail, and frumpy. The type they thought was destined to be single. She was pitiful, in their opinion.

"What is he doing? Does he want to offer a cheap price? A bargain bride?" The villagers were in a quandary. Their speculation turned to shock when the young man offered ten cows to the young maiden's parents. Ten! Her father practically shoved her onto his horse, and the two dashed off for their honeymoon.

A year later when the newlyweds returned, the bride was nearly unrecognizable. Her eyes sparkled, she stood up straight and tall, and her frail figure had filled out. Confident. Glowing. A new beauty. A real looker! Out with Miss Pitiful; in with Lady Pitt!

The value her husband placed on her the moment he offered the high dowry had changed her. His love caused her to believe she was worthwhile. She began to see herself as he saw her, and the results were stunning.

You, my friend, are far more than a ten-cow maiden.

You were purchased with the incredibly high price of Jesus's shed blood, and you belong to God. Take a look for yourself!

For God has **bought you with a great price**. So use every part of your body to give glory back to God, because he owns it.

1 Corinthians 6:20 TLB

He has given you all of the present and all of the future. All are yours, and **you belong to Christ**, and Christ is God's.

1 Corinthians 3:22–23 TLB

It's not about what you've done, but whose you are!
Store this on your mental hard drive!

> Know that the LORD Himself is God;
> It is He who has made us, and not we ourselves;
> We are **His people** and the sheep of His pasture.
>
> Psalm 100:3 NASB

> For you are a holy people, who **belong** to the LORD your God.
>
> Deuteronomy 7:6 NLT

As his daughter, you **belong** to him.

God values you; God loves you. Are you getting it? Are you letting this stuff get to your core and change how you see yourself? Will you let it change your thinking? See, just like the frail, frumpy maiden, if you see yourself the way God sees you, you will believe you have great worth. And the results will be stunning!

These are some mind-boggling truths, but they are just that—true! They are statements and promises inspired by the Holy Spirit to be written in the Bible so that you would know the truth and it would set you free! Think about it. How does knowing you belong to God affect the way you see your worth?

According to John 10:28–29 you **permanently** belong to God. It's not some temporary thing, like as long as you're a sweetie pie who plays by his rules, otherwise you'll be out on your rear. No, not like that. It's a forever thing. Here it is:

> I give them eternal life, and they shall never perish; no one can snatch them out of my hand. My Father, who has given them to me, is greater than all; no one can snatch them out of the Father's hand.
>
> NIV

Forever in the Father's hand, forever in God's grasp! You are part of him, and he is part of you. You belong together. Never to be separated.

So you are securely in God's hand, attached to him and unable to be snatched, stolen, robbed, dropped, or permanently detached from his palm. Simply amazing. I guess when he said he would never leave you or forsake you, he meant it!

# Catching On?

This acceptance thing is a huge issue. It will affect your entire life, so let's make sure you're catching on. Based on what you've read so far, mark these statements T for true or F for false.

____ The Bible says God has chosen you and will not throw you away.

____ God loves you so much that if you were the only person on earth, God still would have sent Jesus to die just for you.

____ Becoming a party girl, like Heidi did, is understandable if you've had a rough life and feel hurt or rejected.

____ Trashing your commitment to abstinence is worth it if the guy fulfills your need to be wanted and accepted.

____ God, through the Bible and his Holy Spirit, can change you.

____ To your heavenly Father, you never have been and never will be unwanted.

____ Your description and suggested price could possibly appear on eBay.

____ When we do wrong, God alone has the right to treat us the way we truly deserve, but because we belong to him, his mercy, grace, and forgiveness are what we get.

____ God knows absolutely everything about you and still loves you.

____ Your acceptance is based not on what you've done, but on whose you are.

# WHaT? no aPPLause?

I was thrilled to have been selected as a member of the *God-spell* cast. From a high school enrollment of more than two thousand and with more than a hundred students trying out, I was shocked that I made it.

I auditioned with my older sister. She was the outgoing one. I was shy. She had the better voice. I was good at smiling! When called into the audition, we were excited. We sang "Wash That Man Right Out of My Hair" from the Broadway musical *South Pacific*. The audition was fun because we were together.

Then we both made the cut. I was thrilled. There were far more talented singers than me who were not selected. However, I could play the guitar. In fact, I shared my part with another girl, Liz, and she could pluck out a few songs as well. The night she sang I accompanied her and vice versa.

After weeks of rehearsals, line memorization, choreography, costume selection, and makeup application, opening night finally arrived. It was a sellout crowd. We were all thrilled. And nervous. A good nervous, but nonetheless nervous.

Opening night I played the guitar while Liz sang. The next night we switched.

My scene approached. I quickly ran the lyrics through my mind for the bazillionth time. My moment arrived.

Let me set the scene for you. First of all, *Godspell* is a musical drama about the life of Jesus as portrayed in the Gospel of Matthew. It's full of parables, so there are lots of stories we acted out. Everyone on the cast played disciples in most scenes.

In my scene, Jesus was turning to walk away from the disciples after a confrontation. They headed upstage; Jesus headed downstage. Then the house lights were cut, and the stage lights were dimmed. Two soft spotlights shone. One on me, one on Jesus. (Jesus was darn cute, by the way. Some guy named Michael who was a football player. Mmm.)

As Jesus was walking away, Liz started strumming her guitar. I took a big breath from deep within my diaphragm and opened my mouth to sing.

Okay, you need to know that I had never even done a solo in choir. I was the shy girl, remember? I wasn't known for belting out the tunes. So singing this song—alone—was risky. I was totally vulnerable. Unmasked. And in front of hundreds of pairs of eyes. I could feel them on me. And it wasn't just *their* eyes, but honestly, I think this was the first time Michael the football king and drama star had ever actually bothered to look at me.

The tension was thick.

With all the courage and emotion I could scrounge up, I began to sing, "Where are you going? Where are you going? Will you take me with you? For my hand is cold and needs warmth, where are you going?" (Yes, take me with you, Michael—oh, um, I mean Jesus.)

The intimate moment between my character and the Master came to a close. The song ended. The guitar stopped.

Then the nightmare occurred.

The audience was silent.

No one applauded.

I'm serious, not even my mom and dad. I thought all parents were **obligated** to clap for their kid. Isn't that a law?

Anyway, Michael/Jesus rushed right into the next scene, and I drifted into a fog. My head was spinning. I was stunned.

*Was I off-key? Out of tune? Did I go flat or maybe sharp? Did I not effectively express the right emotions to match the lyrics? Or did I just plain stink?*

I fought back tears. Breathing deeply over and over and forcing myself to refocus on the scene at hand were the only things that saved me from becoming a little puddle of mush right there, center stage.

No applause.

It's an awful feeling. Has it happened to you? Of course it has. You finally made the cheerleading squad after two years of tryouts, and no one celebrated with you; you won the history project, and no one cared; you made the honor roll, and no one congratulated you; your braces finally came off, and no one noticed; you aced the calculus exam for the first time ever in the history of your school career, and no one gave a flip.

You did your best, you tried harder than before, you were extra creative, you put your heart and soul into something, and then you put yourself out there. But you got next to nothing in return. No "good job," no "great effort," no "atta-girl," no dinner out on the town.

It happens to all of us and will continue to happen (it's a fact of life).

How can we pick ourselves up off the ground, swipe off the dirt and gravel, and keep going (and without being bitter)?

My friend Stacy pushed herself hour after hour, test after test, night after night, just yearning to graduate college magna cum laude. And she did. But the one person she was trying so hard to impress, so hoping to gain the approval of, was her older brother, who was a successful doctor. But he never even congratulated her. Never said a word.

What is a crushed heart to do?

How can we adjust our thinking and get the right perspective?

Here's my hard-learned answer.

Ready?

Change your audience!

# a new audience

In your mind you have an audience. It consists of specific people you hope to please, or at least stay in their good graces. There are others you want to keep from criticizing you or putting you down. This audience has the potential to propel you forward or send you plunging down—but only if you let them. If you catch yourself choosing what you wear, where you will go, who you will talk to, or who you will hang out with based on what a particular person will say, then I pray you will be open to some needed changes. Any time someone is stopping you from accepting yourself or being yourself, change needs to take place or else you risk being unhappy. You risk losing your peace and your joy in life. That isn't God's plan.

So out with the old, in with the new!

Politely usher out those who didn't respond or who responded badly to you, and bring in a new crew. Really.

You can choose to stop living out your life before others who are critical, judgmental, and stingy with their accolades.

Take away their power. Oh yes, they will still be in your auditorium of life, but you can require them to take the seats way in the back. You can force them to sit on the hard bleachers, high in the nosebleed section, where you can barely see them or hear them.

And if you want to boot a few of them out completely, you can. Like that sassy pop girl who always has something nasty to say about your clothes, your brother's buddies who are forever crass around you, or your vocal coach who constantly rolls his eyes when you go sharp. On and on. You know who those people are in your life. They close up your spirit. They shut you down. They can cause you to question yourself and your value. You can choose to weaken the sting of their disapproval.

*Wait, what if they're my immediate family, you know, like my mom or dad or my grandfather? Then what?*

Great question, and I'm glad you brought it up, because we need to chat it out. In all my years of hanging with teen girls, I've heard lots of stories. Take Krista, whose dad cusses her out (including the "F word") over every little thing; Marley, whose mom slaps her face; Erika, whose grandmother constantly calls her "fat a—" and takes her sister places but never her; and Lauren, whose brother has molested her.

Only in extreme cases is it okay to cut off your family members. The Bible has much to say about the value of family and the way we are to treat them. So don't dream about waving good-bye. Instead, dare to turn down their volume. Yes, follow the Bible by continually responding to them with gentleness and kindness, but don't let them trash you, overpower you, or rule your heart.

So what are you to do?

1. **Guard your heart.** How? By mentally catching their words or actions in midair and throwing them over your shoulder so they don't get lodged in your heart.
2. **Shake it off.** In the Bible, the apostle Paul reached down to toss a pile of sticks onto a campfire, and a poisonous snake bit into his hand and didn't let go. Paul shook the snake off—into the fire—and suffered no harm (Acts 28:3–5). My young friends, when you get bit, flick your wrist and refuse to accept it. Don't let the venom seep into your soul. Shake it off, B.A.B.E.!
3. **Forgive and let it go.** It's a matter of choice! Fast-forward to page 98 to get the forgiveness facts.

Need a friend? If you are struggling with abuse, an eating disorder, or a similar situation, here's help just for teen girls:
Mercy Ministries
www.mercyministries.com
615-831-6987

Remuda Ranch
Programs for anorexia and bulimia
www.remuda-ranch.com
800-445-1900

4. **Change your focus.** Take your eyes off the family members (or friends or whoever) who try to boo you off of the stage, and lock eyes with your new audience.

You are responsible before the Lord as to how you treat and act toward others, especially your family. In the end you will answer to God alone. Sounds harsh, but it's true. Do you have to let them crush your spirit, your confidence, your dreams, your hopes? No. Plain and simple. Yet here are the things you do have to do. Read the verses and write the action.

"A **gentle** answer turns away wrath, but harsh words stir up anger."
~ Proverbs 15:1 NLT
Your action:

"Since God chose you to be the holy people whom he loves, you must clothe yourselves with tenderhearted **mercy**, **kindness**, **humility**, **gentleness**, and **patience**. You must **make allowance** for each other's faults and **forgive the person** who offends you. Remember, the Lord forgave you, so you must forgive others." ~ Colossians 3:12–13 NLT
Your action:

"**Never pay back evil for evil to anyone.** Do things in such a way that everyone can see you are honorable. Do your part to live in peace with everyone, as much as possible. Dear friends, never avenge yourselves. Leave that to God. For it is written, 'I will take vengeance; I will repay those who deserve it,' says the Lord. Instead, do what the Scriptures say: 'If your enemies are hungry, feed them. If they are thirsty, give them something to drink, and they will be ashamed of what they have done to you.' Don't let evil get the best of you, but conquer evil by doing good."
~ Romans 12:17–21 NLT
Your action:

# DRASTIC MEASURES

Usher in a new audience.

See the doors swing open and extend a warm welcome. But wait. You see only one figure slowly making his way down the center aisle. You strain to look. *Who is that?*

He slowly comes into view.

His glow gives off warmth that reaches out and draws you in. His presence calms your heart. His love fills your empty places. His acceptance heals the brokenness. His peace replaces your fears. His gentleness lifts your inadequacies. His strength rushes to strengthen your weaknesses. His joy overtakes your sadness.

In his presence you feel so different, yet so natural, so calm, so secure, so safe, so genuine. So you!

Speechless, you continue to watch him.

He smiles as he takes a seat.

First row, in the middle.

That would be front and center!

He sits with his eyes on you, you alone. He sits down. His eyes are glued on you, you alone!

You have his full, undivided attention.

Meet your new audience.

Your audience of One!

Close your eyes and picture it. Then describe what you see, hear, and feel:

## In Her Own Words . . .

When you dance with God, He will do things both in and through you that you never thought you could do. He will do things He isn't doing in and through anyone else. And when you dance for Him alone, He will clap louder than any audience you have ever had.*

~ Shannon Kubiak Primicerio

*Check out this quote in *The Divine Dance*, page 175. Shannon is a graduate of Biola University and penned *The Divine Dance* right out of college! Wow. What a B.A.B.E. she is. Take a look at what she's up to at www.beingagirlbooks.com.

# TWO THUMBS UP

With freedom and ease of movement you begin to live out your life before your God. He smiles. He takes delight in you.

He gives gentle promptings when you forget your lines, he comforts you during the painful scenes, he guides you when you lose your way, he strengthens you when you feel weary, and he leads you the entire way.

Finally the scene ends.

Now you wait. Wait for the comments to come in. Wait for your audience to critique your performance, to analyze your portrayal of your character. To see if you were believable and convincing as you simply played the part of being you.

Ah, the reviews are in. You apprehensively take a peek.

Five stars! A perfect score! Two thumbs up!

*Wait! Even when I feel like my life is a low-budget, no-frills, off-Broadway production? Even when I gave a halfhearted performance? Even when my attitude lagged? Even when I didn't get nominated for a Tony Award, Broadway's highest honor?*

Even then.

The all-time, most highly esteemed critic gives you two thumbs up.

Do you see him? He is so pleased and proud of you. Look! Now he is standing to applaud you! Oh, it's not a polite, quiet little clap; it's a big whompin' smack of his hands. The kind that can rattle heaven and earth. Now look at what he's doing. He is so excited and into you that he's doing the wave. To the right—whoo! To the left—whoo!

He's so over the top, isn't he? But wait—

Did you hear that? I know I heard him say something. Listen.

**"She's fine! She's divine! She's mine!"**

A cheer! He's actually cheering for you. Incredible.

*How can this be?*

Simple. Your new audience doesn't critique you based on your performance, abilities, or achievements. No, his applause is rooted in his love for you and in his joy at being your heavenly Father. Perhaps you're beginning to grasp the full and liberating meaning of the words *unconditional* and *complete*. See, with God as your audience, his acceptance of you is both of these things.

Unconditional. No strings attached. Without limits.

Complete. Lacking nothing. Full. Maximized. Without reservation.

Think about that all day, all week. Let it get inside your soul and become part of you!

**Your heavenly Father knows you by name.**

# Sitting Pretty

Have you ever heard the expression that a person with a good fortune of some sort is "sitting pretty"? It means she is in a good position, seated in a prime spot. She's got it going on! Well, girl, you are sitting pretty!

See, since you belong to God, and since you've put your faith in Jesus, you have a special position. You are now "in Christ." That entitles you to all sorts of rights and privileges. Yet if you don't know who you are in Christ, you won't claim those rights or walk in those privileges. You won't have an accurate assessment of your value and worth. You won't have a realistic self-image. You won't get the full advantage of being you. It would be like an eagle not knowing it's an eagle, so it never learns to fly! Grounded for life, never to become what its maker intended. Don't let that be your story.

It is absolutely imperative that you know and understand who you are as God's child. And where should you look to gather these facts? The Bible, of course!

Why? Because your self-image (the way you see yourself) and your self-esteem (the way you feel about yourself) must be built on a foundation that won't fade out like a trendy fad. The Bible is true, solid, and unchanging! Jesus is the same yesterday, today, and forever. Check it out:

The grass withers, and the flowers fade, but the **word of our God** stands forever.

Isaiah 40:8 NLT

God and his Word are trustworthy! You can bank on it.

So brace yourself. You're about to discover some awesome things about yourself that you may not know, things that will boost your self-image and self-esteem because they are from God. Things that will help you put to rest that all-important question: Who am I? The Bible verses you are about to read are going to rock your identity. They will confirm that you are accepted. But more than that, they will show that you are **acceptable**. Yep, because of Jesus, you are acceptable to God! Here we go! Let your true identity be revealed!

**Everything the Bible says about you is true. It does not change. It cannot lie.**

**You need a new view of you to cancel out an incorrect one!**

# WHO YOU ARE IN CHRIST

(Pssst! Go get your Bible so you can set your baby blues, breathtaking browns, or gorgeous greens on these verses for yourself. I will list them here, but you really need to know where they are in your Bible. Underline or circle them so they jump out at you every time you flip by.)

- You are God's child, adopted into his family as his very own (see Ephesians 1:5; John 1:12). It's the best family ever. You're a full-fledged member, entitled to an inheritance.

- You are born of God, and the evil one cannot touch you (see 1 John 5:18). Oh yeah. You are God's property!

- You are a member of Christ's body (see 1 Corinthians 12:27). You are his hands and feet, his eyes and ears, here to serve.

- You are a partaker of his divine nature (see 2 Peter 1:3–4). You have everything you need to live a godly life.

- You are created in God's likeness (see Genesis 1:26–27). You have his qualities growing in you as you are faithful to seek him.

- You are fearfully and wonderfully made (see Psalm 139:13–14).

Remember, you are not just carelessly tossed together.

- You are chosen by Jesus and called his friend (see John 15:15–16). You are not a slave, not a neighbor, not an acquaintance, but a friend!

- You are the home of the Holy Spirit, who lives in you (see 1 Corinthians 6:19; John 14:16–18). You are more than flesh and bones; you are a hangout for the Holy Spirit.

- You are forgiven (see 1 John 1:9). You are forgiven even when you blow it big-time, even when you do it over and over.

- You are holy (see Ephesians 1:4; 1 Corinthians 3:17). God's Spirit living in you makes you holy! Holy also means to be set apart for God's purposes. That's you!

- You are blameless in God's sight (see Ephesians 1:4). Sounds unimaginable, but because of Jesus, God sees you as faultless!

- You have been bought with a price and belong to Christ (see 1 Corinthians 6:20). Your sins were paid for in full when Jesus died on the cross.

- You are redeemed (see Ephesians 1:14). You've been restored and given new and everlasting value.

- You have the righteousness of God (see 2 Corinthians 5:21). Jesus grants us his righteousness, and we are in right standing with God.

- You are loved (see Ephesians 2:4; John 3:16). Even when it feels like no one else loves you, God always does.

- You cannot be separated from God's love (see Romans 8:35–39). No fear of rejection here.

- You are a brand new creation in Christ (see 2 Corinthians 5:17). God made you new and clean on the inside—totally different.

- You are complete in Christ (see Colossians 2:10). Yep. You have it all—love, peace, security, kindness, joy, power, sound mind . . . You name it, it's yours.

- You are a saint, a citizen of heaven (see 1 Corinthians 1:2–3; Philippians 3:20). This world isn't your real home; you are on loan from the throne!

- You have direct access to God (see Ephesians 2:18). You don't have to use a formula or go through another person to get to God.

- You are God's workmanship, created for good works (see Ephesians 2:10). You're a work of art designed to do good things for Jesus!

- You have eternal life in heaven (see 1 John 5:13). What better place to spend forever?

- You can do all things through Christ who strengthens you (see Philippians 4:13). What God assigns you to do, he will help you through.

- You are free from condemnation (see Romans 8:1–2). Don't let anyone put you down. God has lifted you up!

- You are protected by the power of God (see 1 Peter 1:5; 2 Thessalonians 3:3). Ask and he will send his angels anytime!

- Your adequacy is from God (see 2 Corinthians 3:5). It's not about what you can do, but about what God can do through you!

- You are sealed in Christ by the Holy Spirit of promise (see Ephesians 1:13). Signed, sealed, and eventually delivered to heaven. If Jesus is your Lord, you are headed to heaven. It's a sure thing!

- You have been given a spirit not of fear, but of power, love, and a sound mind (see 2 Timothy 1:7). Forget dread, panic, worry, and timidity. You've got the power.

- You are salt in this world (see Matthew 5:13). Your very presence can make others thirsty for God.

- You are a light in this world (see Matthew 5:14, 16; Ephesians 5:8). Your love and good deeds for God make you shine and point others to the heavenly Father.

- You have been called to bear fruit (see John 15:16). What joy you have when you see God working in and through you.
- You are seated with Christ in the heavenly realm (see Ephesians 2:6). You've got spiritual royalty to the max.
- You have been created with a plan and purpose in mind (see Psalm 139:16; Jeremiah 29:11–13). God has your life mapped out.
- You are victorious through Christ (see Romans 8:37). Victory in Jesus—it's all about obedience.
- You are called to be a witness for Christ and to make disciples (see Mark 16:15; Acts 1:8). What an honor to tell others about Jesus and help them learn his ways.
- You are filled with power from God (see Acts 1:8; Ephesians 3:20). You are never dependent on your own abilities. God's power works in us.
- You have been given authority and power over your enemy, Satan (see 1 John 4:4). God in you (the Holy Spirit) is greater than the god of this world (Satan)! You can tell him what to do (in Jesus's name)!
- You are crowned with glory and majesty (see Psalm 8:3–5). You're a princess glowing with God's glory!

Blown away? Speechless? Overwhelmed? I thought so! Seeing so many of these verses together is amazing. They're all true, and they all apply to you. I want you to do yourself a favor now. Go back through the list and make it personal. In the place of "you are," put "I am." Do it now and read it out loud. This is powerful.

**Take your time—don't rush.** And don't worry about me. I'll wait until you're done. I think I'll go get some popcorn.

Done? Cool. Describe how that felt.

Now I want you to select four truths from the list that impacted you the most.

1.
2.
3.
4.

Great. One more thing. Jot down **why** each of the truths you selected impacted you.

1.
2.
3.
4.

Are you finished? Did you really do it? I can't express to you how important this is.

If you've been told you aren't worth much, that you'll never amount to anything, that you're stupid, that you're a loser, that you aren't good at anything, that God burped when he made you, that you're a disappointment, or whatever, then speaking God's truths about you may have felt weird. They may have challenged what you've been told and what you have believed about yourself. **Only** what **God** says is absolute truth.

Therefore, you'd better read these verses every day so they can get deep within your spirit. Then you can use them like a sword to battle those ugly thoughts (lies) that pop into your mind. Take these verses, make them yours, and use them as a weapon. For instance:

"My life is a mess. I'm such a waste." **Not true!** You are God's workmanship created in Christ. You are complete in him. You have been chosen by God, and he has a specific plan for you to bear fruit and be his witness.

"I sinned again. I blew it, and now God must hate me." **Not true!** You are his child, adopted into his family, forgiven of your sins and always welcome to go boldly and confidently into his presence.

"I must be so disgusting looking, because no guy even talks to me, let alone asks me out." **Not true!** You are fearfully and wonderfully made in the image and likeness of God. He thinks you're the bomb!

"I'll never end up being a pediatrician. I can't even pass this science test. All this study is a waste on my brain." **Not true!** You have the mind of Christ and have been given a spirit of love, power, and a sound mind. God fills your heart with his desires, so you can achieve the dreams he places in your heart.

See how that works? Understand why this is important?

Now you try it. Write down the lies or half-truths the enemy has been whispering in your ear. Then replace them with the things God says about you!

False:

True:


False:

True:


False:

True:

**"Let the words of Christ, in all their richness, live in your hearts and make you wise."** ~ Colossians 3:16 NLT

# Frapuccino FLOPS

When you keep your eyes locked on your new audience and you get a new view of you based on the truth of the Bible, you'll be less likely to seek out approval, attention, or attagirls from other sources. Our natural, human need for approval and acceptance can make us want to get it from almost anywhere just as long as we get it! That need can make us girls do things we wouldn't do if we fully understood and put into practice God's unconditional acceptance of us. See, if you don't comprehend God's acceptance, chances are you're gonna look for it in all the wrong places. You're gonna end up pretending to be something you aren't and doing things you don't really want to do in hopes of being accepted, in hopes of fitting in and belonging. You're gonna be a **frapuccino flop**! On the outside you might appear to be blended together just perfectly, but the inside will be full of the wrong ingredients and you will feel like yuck! It's a bad place to be. You just can't try to fit by changing into someone you aren't! Eventually the front you're putting up will flop. Don't let that happen to you. There are many things girls do in their search for acceptance. Let's look at some. Do you see a hint of yourself anywhere here?

**The Camouflage Queen!** This girl hides her true self. She makes masking her MO (mode of operation) in hopes of being liked by everyone (which is impossible). She becomes a quick-change artist as she strives to be what she perceives others want her to be. She is a people pleaser. She is desperate to blend in. She is ultrainsecure and clueless about who she is as her own person.

**The Druggie Dweller!** This girl gives in to the pressure of drugs and alcohol. Getting high is no longer a back-alley activity reserved for the slime of the earth (though indulging might land you there). It's very mainstream. You know better than I do that drugs and alcohol are easy to obtain. Therefore, nearly every girl (including you) is going to get passed a pill or dared to take a hit or throw back a shot. All eyes stare and wait. Yes, it's intimidating. Going along is the easy thing to do, but it's the worst thing to do, especially since the druggies' acceptance of this girl is based only on her willingness to do as they do. Once she refuses, she's out. She loses her sense of herself and usually walks on thin ice with the pushers and users. It's a dangerous place to be.

**The Compromise Chick!** This girl trashes her beliefs and values to gain or maintain popularity. Being at the top of the social ladder becomes an addiction satisfied only with the drug of flattery. That's false admiration. Popularity always has a price tag. The cost of denying one's own values system is very high as it wreaks havoc on the inside. When a person chooses to behave contrary to what she believes, she loses a sense of peace on the inside; she loses perspective on what is really important. Eventually she is miserable. Certainly, that can't be worth it.

**The Big Flirt!** This girl acts like she's an early graduate of Flirt State University. She excels at pouring on the charm and drawing attention to herself in hopes of capturing the attention of almost anything with testosterone. This is the girl who thinks she is nothing without a guy on her arm, a date to prom, or Saturday night plans. This flirty girl might not be sexually active, but she thrives on the attention of guys, which gives the impression that she is!

**The Diet Diva!** This chica chastises her body with crash diets. Living in a "thin is in" society causes this girl to start the crusade to become a skinnier version of herself. She battles the bulge with starvation diets, restricted eating, bingeing and purging, liquid supplements, and on and on. Eventually she becomes a casualty of the weight war within. If the scale goes up two pounds, she has a bad day, and she verbally downs herself all day. Self-sabotage. If the scale goes down or those jeans feel looser, she's up. Food (and usually exercise) controls her. This girl may develop bulimic eating patterns (binge and vomit) or turn anorexic (forget eating altogether). Fifteen percent of these girls die.

**The "Feel the Burn" Girl!** This girl is a workout or sports maniac who collapses from overtraining. She may actually get physically sick from overexercise and exhaustion. She may have ongoing cold symptoms and fatigue, but the need to be counted among the excellent athletes drives her onward. She believes that being number one will be the thing that validates her. Beating out her competition feeds her inner needs.

**The Dumb-Down Girl!** This girl conceals her intelligence to capsize the smart-girl image. Dumbing down is truly a dumb thing to do, but if someone has been teased about being smart or has the desire to hang with a group that's disgusted with school, she will hide her academic talents. Exclusion seems the worst. But it's not. Burying the brain God has given to be used for good is the true crime.

**The Brainiac!** This girl does just the opposite of the last one. She studies all the time and crams her brain with info in hopes of winning the approval of her peers, her teachers, and the academic community. Or maybe she does it just to get her mom or dad to be proud of her. Meeting their expectations can be the end all. This girl may end up valedictorian of her graduating class and the recipient of scholarships and special awards, yet her real motivation is all about being liked and accepted.

**The Fashion Hottie!** This girl goes for the cheap look. There's no denying that usually the trendiest teen fashions are revealing and sensual. They've been designed to show off the body. Choosing to dress in these immodest styles just to be counted among the fashionable crowd can backfire. Too tight, too low cut, too short, and too bare can be taken too far! It makes a girl look trashy. It gives a slutty impression. Overdoing it in the makeup department can have the same results.

**The Sex Kitten!** This girl eagerly snuggles up in a guy's arms, and perhaps his bed. She gives away various levels of her purity in hopes of proving her worth, in hopes of hanging on to a boyfriend who's about to bolt, in hopes of her classmates noticing she has someone who thinks she's the bomb. This is scary. This sexually active girl can quickly get caught in a mudslide that lands her with a broken heart, a reputation that's hard to change, a pregnancy, or an STD (sexually transmitted disease). These choices have lifetime consequences.

**The Cruel Cutter!** This girl is all about cruel and unusual punishment—toward herself! Though she may not see it as self-punishment, a girl who cuts or burns herself is taking her problems out on herself. This self-mutilation is about inflicting physical pain on the outside in hopes of quieting the inner gnawing she feels due to lack of acceptance. These are hurts that leave visible scars.

Compromising, overachieving, flirting, dieting, cutting—gosh! Girls will do all sorts of things to gain acceptance from others. Their search for approval can cause them to act in ways they wouldn't if they truly knew God's acceptance.

Is this true of you?

My young friend, listen!

Being driven by the desire to make yourself count to someone else is like spinning your wheels in a mud puddle. It's messy and unproductive. Eventually you may lose your footing and fall. Eventually you may lose sight of who you really are.

To varying degrees, each of these girls we identified struggles with feeling worthless, unnoticed, unacceptable, left out, undesirable, or unable to measure up. Do you relate to any of these feelings?

Well, that's got to stop!

That's why we're talking about it right here, right now!

Can you see why gleaning your acceptance from God is so very important? It will keep you from being less than your best and less than what God has planned for you. It will keep you from trying to get acceptance in other ways. It will keep you from acting out or withdrawing from life. Get your unconditional acceptance from God! It will keep your view of yourself from being trampled. It will keep you tracking with God's best for your life.

# BUT I DON'T *FEEL* IT!

*But I don't **feel** very accepted around church or school!*

Acceptance by God and acceptance by peers are two different things.

I'll never forget those wicked Tuesdays and Thursdays in junior high when my class schedule required that I drag myself to P.E.—that's physical education for those of you beyond the generation forced to remove our clothes, change into our dusty blue gym suits, endure fifty minutes of sweat, then strip down along with the sixty other girls in various stages of pubescence to sprint through the showers feeling humiliated! No, wait. There was always a Jezebel in the group who flaunted her naked, full-bloom bosoms in front of us flat-figured girls. She was the only one not humiliated!

Seventh period was my dreaded hour.

I totally detested the "pick me" style of creating sports teams. The team captains, selected by the teacher, would take turns picking team members. The choosing always went from the most athletic to the least.

I was always among the final few uncoordinated athletic wannabes in the class.

It was usually me and Brenda.

This competition for who would be left as the ultimate dweeb had been going on between me and Brenda since the fourth grade. My family had moved from Ohio to Wisconsin in the middle of the school year. I had the honor of being the "new kid." That's never good for a skinny girl wearing lace-trimmed anklets and pink horn-rimmed glasses.

Brenda had glasses too. Hers were blue but much, much thicker! I was clearly the cooler of the two.

Brenda was a foot taller than me and just as skinny. We became the target of a gang of moronlike boys. The worst was the day it had rained and they threw worms in our faces. I didn't know if I should hate school, the boys, Brenda, or myself.

Truly, I didn't get it. Other than being shy, I was a friendly girl who loved reading, crafts, and playing the guitar. Of course, no one ever bothered to find that out at the time. Ever been there?

Anyway, off this soapbox and back to P.E.!

The feeling of standing there holding my breath while hoping and praying someone—anyone—would pick me to be on their team always left me feeling like, well, leftovers! Like a cold pan of lasagna that hadn't been consumed the first time around and now had to be dished out onto the plate because there was no other choice. I'll bet Brenda felt it too.

Leftovers.

These feelings lingered until my late high school years when I started to excel in art and drama. My paintings hung in the school hallways, and I was appointed student director for our musical, *The Sound of Music*. Then I was selected to represent my school as a model for a local department store. Later I was a finalist in the Wisconsin Junior Miss Scholarship Pageant. Sweet. My name appeared on the list of Top 20 Girls in my class of 524. I was featured in the school newspaper. My artwork was moved to the front lobby. At last others noticed that perhaps I had notable worth and value after all. I was finally on the road to acceptance. I could feel it.

But what if those feelings never came? That is exactly why you and I need an audience of One! God's acceptance is not a consolation prize—it is the prize!

Not one of us likes the feeling of being picked over, looked over, or ignored. No one rejoices over rejection.

# RAUNCHY REJECTION

In some way **all of us** experience rejection. Friends ditch us, parents make stinging comments that get cemented into our brains, we don't get invited to the big bash, our name isn't on the honor roll, a friend betrays our trust, we lose a class election, we get cut from a team, we get dumped by a guy. We've all been there.

The crummy part is that if we experience rejection over and over, we might just decide we are rejects, losers, that we have nothing to offer and will never amount to anything. We aren't good enough, smart enough, fast enough, attractive enough, rich enough, or cool enough. Just not enough!

When and why have you felt this way?

I watched *The Wedding Planner* on TV recently. The scene was one we would all want to avoid. Mary, played by Jennifer Lopez, is at an open-air floral market with a client named Steve, played by Matthew McConaughey, when she runs into her ex-fiancé, who is now married to her ex–best friend. They are both *ex* because Mary found them making out in her car the night before the big wedding. Crushing! Later we see a crying and depressed Mary beating herself up over the breakup and concluding that she couldn't keep her fiancé because she just wasn't enough. The handsome, caring, compassionate Steve strokes her face, reassuring her that that isn't true. (Wouldn't we all like *him* to show up every time we're feeling blue?) Naturally, we think that someone like the real Jennifer Lopez has never really felt like rejected leftovers. Not true. Especially when a person has been through as many men as J.Lo has. Cris Judd. Rapper Puff Daddy or P. Diddy, or Poo Witty, or whatever. Okay, I know it's Sean "Puffy" Combs. Then Ben Affleck. Then Marc Anthony. And those are just the men to date. Believe me, she's been rejected. In fact, she's been rejected so much that she's become an expert at rebounding right into the arms of another guy. That helps hide the pain of rejection, but it's still there.

Feeling like we're not enough.

We might find ourselves pulling away from others, hanging back, choosing to stop showing up at youth group, quitting a team, or slacking off on life!

But what if the conclusions we draw about ourselves are inaccurate? What if we're wrong? What if the people who acted badly toward us were just having a bad day, a bad week, or a bad life? What if the way they acted wasn't even about us? It was about them. Who are you going to let influence your decision about your value, your worth? Girlfriends? Classmates? Casual acquaintances? Guys? Teachers? Coaches? Parents? Friends? Foes? Movies? Magazines?

Putting too much stock in others' offhanded comments or opinions could cause your self-image to plummet straight down into a depression. Don't let it happen. Your self-image is too valuable to allow it to be so vulnerable. Protect it with the Bible!

And let me say it again. Focus on what God says about you. He is your audience now, right? Right.

# Blast Out the Blues

During your teen years, you might struggle with feeling sad, down in the dumps, or just plain depressed. It's pretty normal. Put these ideas into practice to help lift yourself up. You can learn to cope in completely positive ways—no self-defeating cop-outs allowed.

1. **Pray it out!** Talk to the Lord, telling him everything. Let him have your worries (1 Peter 5:7). After all, he is the only one who can do anything about most of it!
2. **Write it out!** Use a journal to pour out your thoughts and feelings. Getting it out of you can help you evaluate and move ahead. Then record the things that give you joy. Focus on those.
3. **Talk it out!** Grab a soda or a latte with an older (spiritually and chronologically) Christian. Tell her what's going on. She may have wonderful advice or insight to share.
4. **Speak it out!** What are you saying about yourself or the situation inside your private thoughts? Choose to use positive and truthful self-talk.
5. **Work it out!** Exercise! It releases healthy hormones into your body that help you think clearly and get a fresh perspective.
6. **Hear it out!** Listen to your feelings and emotions. Depression or anger is telling you something is wrong. You may develop physical symptoms like headaches, fatigue, body aches, and reoccurring colds. Pinpoint the problem and get help.
7. **Stomp it out!** Try these: read the Bible, get enough sleep, eat healthy, get with a friend who makes you laugh, watch a funny show, take a warm bath, cry, do something for someone else, let go of shoulds and if only's, forgive those who have hurt you. Do **not** turn to drugs, alcohol, withdrawal, violence, running away, or screaming at others. These actions will add to your blues!

If you have a prolonged sense of sadness (over two weeks) that you can't seem to beat, you may need to see a doctor or a Christian counselor.

# WEEDS

Haley was in the youth group when my husband and I arrived to serve at a church in California. She was a tall blonde with a glowing smile who loved to dress sorta "out there." Fashion was her passion. She challenged things that were considered normal and liked carving out her own way. And she was fun. This girl could make me laugh! From singing silly songs at the top of her lungs to acting out her favorite movie scene, Haley was just Haley.

That's why I was so puzzled when I heard about her past. Haley was born to an unwed mother. She got shifted back and forth between her mom's place and her dad's parents' house. Her mom got into drugs, couldn't hold down a job, and started disappearing for days or weeks at a time. Eventually Haley was permanently given to her grandparents. They had official custody. Her mother told her she didn't want to be her mom anymore, and she took off. Haley's dad wasn't around much either.

Disowned by her mom. Uninteresting to her dad. Handed over to her grandparents, who never expected to raise another child. How would you react if you were Haley? Angry or resentful? Dejected or withdrawn? Rebellious or apathetic? Maybe you would expect Haley to be the kind of girl who gets into trouble. Maybe the kind of girl with a huge chip on her shoulder. Maybe the kind of girl who bullies other girls due to the hurt in her life, or maybe a shrinking-violet kind of girl who is afraid to assert herself.

Instead, as I've gotten to know her, I've learned that she is a confident, caring, tenderhearted young woman. She is secure in herself, able to be a true individual who wears wacky clothes and gets crazy with her girlfriends. Why is that?

Her grandparents did something her mom never would have done. They

## In Her Own Words . . .

Just like other Mean Girl tactics, name-calling is used to make you mad. So the number one thing you have to remember is, **don't let her see you sweat**. Don't react, or at least react totally differently than she expects you to. When you get hurt and retaliate, she wins, plain and simple. So hold your tongue unless you have something nice or funny to say.*

Hayley DiMarco

> * Hey, this quote is from Hayley's book *Mean Girls* (check page 25). Get all the mean girl juice at www.meangirls.net.

took her to church. As a junior higher, Haley began to grow stronger by reading the Bible nearly every day. She hooked up with a group of girls who were Christians. She built her life on Jesus. Deep down she knew he loved her and that he would always be there for her. She counted on him. He was her foundation, her security, her rock.

She didn't let her absentee parents or rude comments from other kids about her living with her grandparents trash how she felt about herself. She focused on Jesus and guarded her heart by weeding out the bad and hanging on to the good.

You can do the same! Yes, you're going to get slammed, dissed, and disowned, so how are you going to react? Try it Haley's way. Start weeding.

Write down the things Haley did to fight off and overcome the rejection in her life:

(There were five of them. Did you get them all?)

Each of these actions is totally doable. Trust Jesus and trust yourself.

It's a tough thing to do. Following Jesus isn't for sissies! He calls us to walk the high road, the narrow road. He calls us to do as he did. Listen up.

> To this you were called, because Christ suffered for you, leaving you an example, that you should follow in his steps. "He committed no sin, and no deceit was found in his mouth." When they hurled their insults at him, he did not retaliate; when he suffered, he made no threats. Instead, he entrusted himself to him who judges justly.
>
> 1 Peter 2:21–23 NIV

When others were mean and rotten to him, Jesus didn't seek revenge. He didn't do the wrong thing, he didn't spread gossip or lies about his offenders, he didn't threaten to take them down! No. In other words, Jesus forgave and let it go. He chose to do the right thing and trust God to take care of the rest. How did he do that? Perhaps it was because he didn't take the rejection personally.

You and I can do the same thing. Rough? Yes. Impossible? No. Jesus doesn't ask us to do things that aren't doable. That would be setting us up for failure. He isn't like that. Just the opposite. He leads by example, then empowers us to follow suit.

Sometimes the raunchy way classmates treat you or the verbal slams they send your way isn't about you at all, but about them. Think about it before you take it personally!

# SORTING THROUGH THE VOICES

Hey, girlfriend, put up a mental screen to sift comments and remarks through. Use it like a grid to embrace the helpful and ban the hurtful. Use it like a screen to first determine the position of the person in your life who is voicing his or her opinion. If he or she is a member of your immediate family or a super-close friend, the comment will carry more weight than that of a casual acquaintance.

Then decide if the person's remarks should be taken seriously. Did she say something totally false, half-true, or totally true?

Should you listen to her or let it go?

Was she really just kidding?

If you decide there's nothing positive or constructive in what she said, kiss it good-bye. That means you need to be the mature one and forgive her. Then forget it.

Okay, easier said than done, but 100 percent possible. You have been forgiven, so you need to forgive.

For if you forgive men when they sin against you, your heavenly Father will also forgive you. But if you do not forgive men their sins, your Father will not forgive your sins.

Matthew 6:14–15 NIV

Yikes. This is serious stuff! You **have to** forgive. It will melt barriers and allow you to love those who have hurt you. **Love?** Yes! Love your enemies and pray for those insensitive jerk dirtbags who persecute you—that's basically what Jesus said to do (see Matthew 5). Ask for God's power to help you forgive. He can and will give you the ability to forgive. Ask for his healing power to touch you, making you whole. Ultimately, let the Bible influence how you feel about yourself (the full scoop on this is coming up). The Bible, God's opinion, is absolute truth!

Now, how observant are you? Did you catch the five instructions I just gave you? You need to! See if you can pinpoint them.

1. _____
2. _____
3. _____
4. _____
5. _____

Rejection and forgiveness must go hand in hand. Otherwise, you take the risk of becoming bitter. Bitterness blasts a beautiful heart. Bitterness is like poison to your system. Get rid of it here and now! Tell the Lord how you feel, who you need to forgive, and ask him to help you:

Now, as an act of your will (even if you don't feel like it yet), choose to forgive. This might be hard, yet it's so important for your emotional, physical, mental, and spiritual health! Ready? Take a deep breath and go for it.

Fill in the blanks with the name(s) of those you need to forgive.

Lord, I choose to forgive _____
for _____

Lord, I choose to forgive _____
for _____

Lord, I choose to forgive _____
for _____

Lord, I choose to forgive _____
for _____

Did you do it? Are your blanks filled in? Is there someone whose name you just couldn't write because you don't even want to see it on paper? Trust me, just writing that name in the blank will be your first step toward forgiving that person, releasing the hurt or hatred you might feel, and breaking that person's power over you. Do it for yourself. You are so worth it. Don't let anyone have a hold on you—except Jesus, of course.

So do you need to keep going? Got more people to forgive? Keep it going on a separate piece of paper. You won't be wasting the time it takes. Do this for Jesus, and do it for you!

# Your View of You

**Hey, girls, what has affected the way you see yourself?**

"Letting go of my need to impress everyone."

~ Heather

"Growing closer to Christ by talking with him daily and studying his Word."

~ Kelly

"Knowing I am forgiven! Yes, sometimes I totally mess up, I let someone down, or I disobey God, or my mom gets mad at me. So knowing God forgives me keeps me from dogging myself."

~ Rachel

"When I hang with the more popular and super-skinny girls, I feel lumpy and out of shape. But when I'm with the more typical girls, I like me. So whoever I surround myself with really affects how I see myself."

~ Lynne

"My friends and I have made a pact to encourage and compliment each other daily. It helps all of us to look to the positive things about ourselves and to challenge each other to be and do our best."

~ Brenda

"When others fail me, I remind myself perhaps it's something in their life that caused them to act that way. It's not always something I did."

~ Lacy

"Deciding to place my self-image on facts, not feelings, has meant everything. My emotions bounce all over the place, so I focus on facts. Like, I'm a nice person, I make good grades, I can place a mean kick on a soccer ball, I'm helpful, and things like that."

~ Mindy

"Trying not to get caught up in the here and now, keeping life in perspective."

~ Kim

"I get affected by which guys like me or think I'm cute. It's easy to fall into that and let it control you. But I'm learning to stay in God's Word and let him set my twisted thoughts straight."

~ Shondra

"Knowing how much God loves me."

~ Angela

"This might sound weird, but learning good manners and how to dress appropriately for each occasion has helped me view myself in a positive light."

~ Brandi

"My current self-image is paradoxical. I know I am a broken, weak vessel and that my only strength comes from a mighty God. However, I also realize that he has crafted me together with the looks, talents, and abilities that he desires, and I rest in his infinite wisdom."

~ Kristie

Is it just reactions from others that threaten to dictate our self-image and personal value?

Nope. Experiences do too. The good ones, the bad ones, and the ugly ones.

Jenna had looked long and hard for a job she could pour herself into. The day she read "small family-owned health-food store looking to hire clerks concerned with health and helping customers" was her break-through day.

Her eyes scanned it again and again. Her heart skipped. She loved food (what teen girl doesn't) and even cared about eating well. And service? She could offer friendly assistance to anyone who entered her domain. She was good at helping others. Thankfully, both she and the manager thought she was perfect for the position!

Three weeks into it Jenna had learned a wealth of information on vitamins, organic foods, whole-grain nutrition, and the difference between good fats and bad fats. She loved helping customers in their search to select the best products to match their needs. Whether it was skin care, juices, or java, she was in the know.

# THE GOOD, THE BAD, AND THE UGLY

She especially loved handing out the samples of products provided by various companies. There were tons of moisturizer, soap, perfume, energy bar, and herbal tea samples. Seeing others delight in a free sample made her feel like every day was Christmas. In fact, when her youth pastor asked students to collect trial-size products for the homeless shelter "Share and Care" project, she was pumped. Boxes of sample size items danced through her head. She knew exactly where she could get her hands on them. She talked to the assistant manager, who thought it was a cool idea too.

The next night at the close of her shift, Jenna collected hundreds of various samples to donate to the shelter. *How sweet to be part of this*, she thought.

But *sweet* was not the word the store owner used when he discovered that tons of the customers' samples had vanished. He had very little to pass out to the shoppers and use to promote his products and increase their purchases! Fewer samples resulted in fewer sales!

After questioning the employees, he found out what Jenna had done. He went to her and demanded the return of the samples. Too late. They were already in the hands of the homeless.

Jenna got fired. Harsh, huh?

She thought she was doing a helpful and loving thing, but her boss saw it very differently, so she got canned. "But the assistant manager said it was okay," she pleaded to no avail. His mind was made up.

Fair? Not really.

But what's a girl to do?

Well, how about feeling good that her intentions were right even if it turned out so wrong? How about forgiving her boss even though he refused to see it from her perspective? How about not holding it against herself and chalking it up to learning that it is always best to check with upper management? How about taking the high road and actually thanking her boss for the opportunity to work at his store even though things didn't end as she had hoped? (It takes a true B.A.B.E. to do that!)

How about praying it through? Let me explain.

Sometimes you'll find yourself experiencing stuff you can't control, stuck in a circumstance you can't change or rearrange. You didn't choose it, but you can't change it. Here again you can take the high road and use it as an opportunity to pray, asking God to help you accept the circumstance in which he seems to have placed you. Ask him to open your eyes to the purpose in the situation, to take what you've been given and somehow make it great.

Wouldn't that be better than doing the opposite? You know, deciding you're a major mess up, a loser, and that life just rots. That kind of conclusion will make your self-image bottom out. That would put you on the low road, the one that leads to negative thoughts, bad attitudes, and blaming of others.

Not good. And not worth it.

We are responsible for our actions and reactions in life, yet we cannot control everything that occurs!

Would it be wise to allow stuff that happens—especially things outside of your control—to determine your self-worth and value? That's putting a bunch of power in potentially the wrong place. The results may be explosive.

Let's get real. If your parents have split, it wasn't your fault. If your grandma dies or someone close to you is suffering from a serious illness, it's not your fault. If at semester break you get a new teacher who doesn't believe in grading on a curve, it's not your doing. If you get a flat tire and end up being three hours late for work, is it your fault? No! If when you open your violin case to tune up right before the citywide recital, you discover a broken string and you don't have a backup and you don't participate, does it make you a loser? No! If your cell phone is stuck in your jammed locker and you don't know your mom has called six times to tell you to pick up your little sister after school, it's just an experience gone wrong. And what about twisting your ankle before the tournament

or accidentally deleting your term paper?

I could go on for the next twelve pages, but I won't. I'll assume you're getting the point. Now, if your SAT scores were in the toilet, or you kept forgetting to feed your bird and it died, or you were chronically late to your babysitting job, or you were grounded because you blew off the note your dad left you asking you to mow the grass, then you'll have to deal with the consequences of stuff you could control.

But often it's a question of perspective. A question of whose perspective you're going to use to influence your decision about your value, your worth, and the way you see yourself. Will it be other people's? Your experiences? Or God's?

By now I hope you answer correctly.

# COURAGEOUSLY CONFIDENT

Okay, a quick time-out! I want you to skim back through this entire section, "A is for Accepted!" in preparation for my upcoming question. Go ahead. Start flipping back through the pages now.

Done?

Great. Here's my question. On a scale of 1 to 10, how accepted do you see yourself?

(low) 1 2 3 4 5 6 7 8 9 10 (high)

My prayer is that you feel totally accepted by your heavenly Father and are on the road to totally accepting yourself! That's right, you're free to be the real deal, the real you. I pray you realize your acceptance can't just be based on feeling! It's a fact from the Bible. I also pray that your newfound acceptance will give you a solid foundation in life, thus allowing you the confidence and freedom to be you!

- Confident because of your connection with Christ!

- Confident that you can do all things through Christ who gives you strength to do and be everything he says in the Bible!

- Confident that you can come boldly into God's throne room of grace, where you will be welcomed with open arms. Whether you come saying, "Hello, Father. I'm so bummed. I need to talk," or "Hey, Father. Guess what awesome thing happened today?" you are forever welcomed.

- Confident because of who God says you are!

- Confident to be who he has created you to be!

- Confident to stand up straight with your head held high, your shoulders back, and a smile on your face and say, "I am accepted, I belong, I am valuable. God loves me!"

**Whoo-hoo!** (Do I hear a Whoo-hoo?)

Suddenly it won't matter so much if you don't fit with the jocks or the drama team. It won't feel the same when someone ditches you or your parents keep fighting. It won't have the same sting when you're teased for taking a stand for abstinence and for not "putting out." Blowing the cheerleading tryouts or being last to be chosen for that sports team won't pack the same punch! You are no longer living under the expectations of others, the results of your experiences, or chaos over the circumstances you can't control.

Confidence is the result of understanding that you are accepted.

This is the kind of confidence that makes a young woman radiantly beautiful! It gives you a glow from the inside out.

**The A in B.A.B.E. is for accepted.** No question about it. You are accepted.

So go ahead. You glow, girl!

# The B.A.B.E. Checklist

Just how accepted are you? Well, totally! By God, that is! We've covered a lot of ground together, but one thing is for sure, girlfriend: God is the Acceptor and you are the acceptee. But do you live it? Have you claimed his singular acceptance of you in your heart? Now that you know how God measures your value and worth, let's see how you measure it in your heart.

| Yes | No | Almost | |
| --- | --- | --- | --- |
| ____ | ____ | ____ | I understand that God fully accepts me with no strings attached. |
| ____ | ____ | ____ | God is my sole audience. |
| ____ | ____ | ____ | I am letting go of my desire to fit in with certain girls in order to feel accepted. |
| ____ | ____ | ____ | I resist the temptation to search for personal acceptance from someone else or someplace else besides the Lord. |
| ____ | ____ | ____ | I will not allow circumstances outside of my control to shatter my self-worth and value. |
| ____ | ____ | ____ | When I feel stung by the words of others, I remember to change my audience to the one whose Word is always true. |
| ____ | ____ | ____ | I allow God's total acceptance of me to influence my acceptance of others. |
| ____ | ____ | ____ | I see that because of my relationship with Jesus, I am worth it. |
| ____ | ____ | ____ | I can confidently say that I am priceless; my value is off the charts. |
| ____ | ____ | ____ | I am feeling and acting more secure and confident in Christ. |
| ____ | ____ | ____ | When a difficult situation comes along, I ask God to help me sort through it, to see it from his perspective. |
| ____ | ____ | ____ | I am beginning to see changes in myself as I rely less on others' approval of me. I am freer to be myself. |
| ____ | ____ | ____ | If someone asked me why I trust God so much, I could answer the question by sharing the living reality of his Word. |
| ____ | ____ | ____ | I can confidently answer the question, "Who am I in Christ?" |

So how'd you do? Does your face shine with his acceptance, or do you need to add a little more of his makeup? Do your words sprinkle his love on others, or has your sparkle kit lost its glitter? If you need to change a "no" or an "almost" into a solid "yes," you know who to ask for help, don't you? That's right! Our Father God. No one can ever take him away from you. He has chosen you. You belong. You are accepted. You are beautiful. Hey, girlfriend, you are beautiful and accepted!

# B IS FOR

# BLES

# SED!

# Blessed? it means, umm . . .

Hmm. It shows up in prayers. At church. In testimonies from Christians you know. But what does it really mean?

Let's take a few minutes to interview some teen girls from around the world—well, from around the food court at the mall, anyway—to see if we can get a solid definition of what it means to be blessed. Help me out, okay? I'll run the video camera to oh so skillfully catch their expressions. You take the microphone, play the role of "teen on the street," and catch their words. Let's see what we come up with.

Look. There are two girls in line over at TCBY. Let's go grab their opinions.

**TOS (that's short for teen on the street):** "Excuse us. We have a question for you: What does it mean to be blessed?"

**Girl #1:** "It's like when you get something you want, like when I talked my parents into letting me go on the ski retreat. Sweet."

**Girl #2:** "I think blessed is something about religion. Like the universe is smiling down on you. Like you're favored and special."

Interesting. Get what you want. A smiling universe (what does that mean?).

Okay, now let's head on over to that group of chicas by Taco Bell. They look like they'll have something to say. Ready? Roll the tape!

**Taco Chica #1:** "Blessed? As in 'bless you'? That's easy. It's just a thing you say when someone sneezes all over the place. Like *gesundheit*—that's the German word for it. Try saying it with an accent. It's so cool. Do you want to hear the French word for—"

Quick, to the next girl, puuleeeeze!

**TC #2:** "I think blessed is when you feel happy and you're in a great mood."

**TC #3:** "Maybe it's like being lucky."

**TC #4:** "Yeah, like when you're given something you didn't ask for."

**TC #5:** "Well then, I mostly know about *not* being blessed. My older brother dogs on me all the time. I hate it."

Wow! Opinions sure do vary! Did you think we'd get such a wide range of answers? I'm feeling sorry for that last girl with the mean brother!

Hey, check out that girl over there with her mom (teen girls who hang with their moms are my heroes). They're totally digging on those Cinnabons! Anyone who eats those sweet treats is a soul sister of mine. I especially love the pecan ones. The caramel icing is luscious.

**Oh, stop poking me!** I only got carried away for a sec. Sugar will do that to me. Let's head over there to hear what she has to say. By the way, do you know you really look cool on camera? Ever thought about being a real reporter? Okay, here you go.

**Cinnabon Girl:** "I know what blessed means. It's when you learn to be okay with life no matter what happens. I know this will sound dramatic, but it's true. See, last year the roof on our house caught on fire and burned all the way through to our living room. Really. We weren't home, but the neighbors saw it and called the firemen, who then drenched the house with water. It was a big mess. We had to move into a tiny apartment while the repairs were being done. Then my mom lost her job, huh, Mom? We ran low on money and ate tons of bologna sandwiches and PB and Js! Well, some people in our church found out and actually had a fundraiser for us. That was unbelievable. But then I caught pneumonia and had to go to the hospital. I told you it was a drama! Without a job, my mom didn't have health insurance, so lots of the money from the fundraiser went to the hospital bill. But here's the thing. I got better quickly, we had the money to pay the bill, Mom got a new job, the miniature apartment grew on us, and we actually hated to leave! We were just fine being there. It's like all of the stuff we really needed, we had—each other, food, shelter, medical care, and a wonderful church. We got to where we were okay with whatever happened, and we chose to be thankful. That's a great place to be. That's a blessing. Everything didn't go our way, but we believe it went God's way."

Gosh! Did you catch that? Being okay with life as it comes because you trust God! That's huge! Instead of blaming God for the unexpected (and unwelcome) situations, they kept a positive attitude and made a conscious effort to be thankful. They made the choice to rejoice. Incredible. Buy that girl another Cinnabon!

Well, let's keep going. I'll bet those chicks drinking lattes will have something to say. They look like seniors. Seniors always have something to say, which is a good thing since they're about to be launched out into the world. Let's go. You first.

**Savvy Senior #1:** "Blessed? Like bliss?"

**SS #2:** "No, blessed is more heartfelt, not just being out-of-your-mind bouncy and thrilled."

**SS #3:** "It's getting into the college you wanted!"

**SS #4:** "It's your weird cousin calling to say he can't come to your graduation party—that was a totally good thing."

**SS #5:** "Well, I feel blessed when someone tosses some encouraging words my way."

See, what did I tell you? Seniors have opinions!

Well, that wraps up our opinion poll. Thanks for your help. But wait! What about you? I'll roll the tape *and* hold the microphone. It's your turn to answer!

To be blessed means:

So far we can conclude that some people think being blessed means being okay with life, having heartfelt happiness like deep inner joy, getting something you didn't ask for—something like a gift—being favored, being encouraged, and having things go God's way.

Before we draw any final conclusions, though, we need to consult the Bible. Yes, I saved the best for last! Check out a few verses.

> God **blesses** those who are persecuted because they live for God, for the Kingdom of Heaven is theirs. God **blesses** you when you are mocked and persecuted and lied about because you are my followers. Be happy about it! Be very glad! For a great reward awaits you in heaven.
>
> Matthew 5:10–12 NLT

> Live in such a way that God's love can **bless** you as you wait for the eternal life that our Lord Jesus Christ in his mercy is going to give you.
>
> Jude 21 NLT

> But **blessed** are those who trust in the LORD and have made the LORD their hope and confidence.
>
> Jeremiah 17:7 NLT

> Jesus replied, "But even more **blessed** are all who hear the word of God and put it into practice."
>
> Luke 11:28 NLT

Wow. These verses shed a different light on things.

Apparently, real blessings flow our way based on how we live our lives—trusting God, living for him, and doing what the Bible says—even when we get pressured, talked about, or teased for being a goody-goody! Real blessings aren't about accumulating stuff like CDs, trophies, clothes, laptops, or whatever you personally covet. And real blessings aren't about popularity, power, or position. Striving to be the queen of a clique, class president, or magna cum laude won't deliver the deep inner satisfaction that comes with a blessing from God. And real blessings are available to each of us! Therefore, you are blessed!

**The B in B.A.B.E. is for blessed!**

# A Different Kind of Blessing

Jesus doesn't promise that life will be a cakewalk. But he does promise to be with us and to provide us with everything we need spiritually. Take a look.

> Praise be to the God and Father of our Lord Jesus Christ, who has blessed us in the heavenly realms with every **spiritual blessing** in Christ.
>
> Ephesians 1:3 NIV

Spiritual blessings! You, my babe-a-licious young friend, are completely and undeniably blessed . . . spiritually!

The blessings I want to chat with you about right now go way beyond your moods or your tally of good versus bad things. They aren't about what you own or what you've earned. They're blessings that come straight from the throne room of God!

A true understanding of these blessings can make all the difference. And because of these blessings, you can never again—no, never—say that you aren't blessed.

So take a stretch break and grab a handful of almonds and a big glass of water (you need eight glasses a day, you know). We've got a lot to talk about!

---

**Real blessings aren't about popularity, possessions, power, or position,**

**but they are all about trusting God and living by his Word.**

# SPIRITUAL BLESSINGS

Are you wondering what makes certain blessings spiritual? Let me help you with that. Here's the scoop: First, spiritual blessings are from God. Second, they're given freely at the time of your second birth (when you accept Jesus and the Holy Spirit into your life), because you belong to God. Third, they have lasting value. They don't show up and then make a quick exit. Fourth, they can't be taken away from you. They're yours to keep for eternity. Fifth, they can make a difference in your life and the lives of those around you. Sixth, they lead to abundant life—the genuine kind! Spiritual blessings aren't about clothes, cars, DVDs, eating out, or getting your nails done. The abundance spiritual blessings bring is about inner peace, true joy, lasting contentment, and so on. Authentic things!

An enormous number of blessings can be called spiritual. But for now we're going to zoom in on my top four favorites! Get ready to be blessed.

## 1. The Blessing of Jesus

You might think of Jesus as God's Son, the Messiah, the leader of a ragamuffin group of guys, the superpower who raised some Lazarus guy from the dead. But a blessing? It may be a new thought, but oh, what a good one! Check it out. God's incredible love for us sent Jesus here to earth to live a sinless life so that he would be qualified to pay the price of our guilty verdict, our death sentence. (All sin is punishable by death. That's why Jesus is soooo important.) Jesus died in our place. He makes it possible for us to become part of God's family. He makes it possible for us to receive all the other spiritual blessings that our Father-God wants to give us. Jesus is our number one spiritual blessing, and he is the one who opens the door to tons more. For instance, salvation! My friend, if you have the blessing of salvation, you can never say that you aren't blessed. You can never say that God hasn't done anything for you. Pause for a second so this can sink in. Pretty amazing, huh?

## 2. The Blessing of Forgiveness

The Bible says all of us are guilty of messing up and doing wrong things. Nobody's perfect. That little anxious feeling you get when you've done something you know is wrong is God working through your conscience—poking at you because you violated a rule. Even if nobody else knows you've done it, your conscience knows.

When you ignore one of your parents' rules, what happens when they find out? If you violate a traffic regulation and get caught, there goes a hunk of your allowance. By far the most serious violation is to break one of God's rules. Yet he's a lot more lenient than your parents or the cop who caught you crawling through a stop sign. All you have to do is plead guilty and fall on the mercy of his "court" and he blesses you with forgiveness. When you ask, he wipes the record clean—as white as snow. He promised!

> Come, let's talk this over! says the Lord; no matter how deep the stain of your sins, I can take it out and make you as clean as freshly fallen snow. Even if you are stained as red as crimson, I can make you white as wool! If you will only let me help you, if you will only obey, then I will make you rich!
>
> Isaiah 1:18–19 TLB

You know how it feels when your hair is super dirty? It looks darker and feels heavier and is sort of plastered to your head. But you jump in the shower, lather it, rinse it, dry it, and then how does it feel? Clean and light and moving freely again.

That's what God's forgiveness is like. It makes you feel clean and light and free. It's a blessing that fills you with thankfulness and joy!

## 3. The Blessing of Eternal Life

This third blessing is almost indescribable! This is how it works. The first time we realize our need for God (maybe for you it was a Christian friend's lifestyle, a youth group retreat, or maybe even The B.A.B.E. Seminar™), we respond by admitting our uh-ohs (sins) to him. Then we ask Jesus to forgive us and come into our lives. That's when we start a personal relationship with him. That's when Jesus opens the door to **all** the spiritual blessings God has for us. That's when we receive our salvation (saved from the punishment of our sins and forever in hell) and are made new on the inside (spiritually born again). That's when God accepts us into his family and blesses us with the opportunity to spend forever with him in heaven! This means that when we die we know where we'll go! No mystery! No doubts! No fears! Wow! In God's presence forever! I can't wait.

What about you? Do you have this special blessing in your life? If not, we must have a B.A.B.E.-to-B.A.B.E. chat right now! There's no way I want you to miss out! Let's talk it through.

1. Do you believe there is a God who made you and loves you? _____ Yes _____ No

"For God so loved the world that he gave his one and only Son, that whoever believes in him shall not perish but have eternal life." ~ John 3:16 NIV

2. Do you believe that Jesus is God's Son, sent to die for your sins? _____ Yes _____ No

"If you confess with your mouth, 'Jesus is Lord,' and believe in your heart that God raised him from the dead, you will be saved." ~ Romans 10:9 NIV

3. Do you admit that you have sinned and need Jesus, the Savior? _____ Yes _____ No

"For all have sinned and fall short of the glory of God." ~ Romans 3:23 NIV

4. Are you ready to turn away from your sins and live to honor God? _____ Yes _____ No

"Repent, then, and turn to God, so that your sins may be wiped out." ~ Acts 3:19 NIV

# FOREVER WITH THE FATHER

5. Are you ready to invite Jesus into your life to be your personal Savior and to become a child of God? _____ Yes _____ No

"But to all who believed him and accepted him, he gave the right to become the children of God. They are reborn! This is not a physical birth resulting from human passion or plan— this rebirth comes from God." ~ John 1:12–13 NLT

If you answered "No" to any of these questions, please find a Christian adult who can help you work through the questions and concerns you may have. This is important stuff that you need to understand. It's a matter of life and death!

If you answered "Yes" to all of these questions, you're ready to pray! Here is a prayer for you to pray out loud with a sincere heart. When you do, God will give you this great bless-

**If you have eternal life, you can never, ever say that you aren't blessed!**

ing and more! Go for it! (You can put this prayer in your own words if you want.)

Holy God, I believe that Jesus is your Son, sent from heaven to die on the cross in my place so he could rescue me from eternal death and give me eternal life. I admit that I need forgiveness of my sins. Jesus, I ask you now to forgive me and invite you to come into my heart to be my personal Savior. Father, send your Holy Spirit into me to manage my life from this day forward. Thank you and I love you!

Signature _____
Date _____

Congratulations! Toss some confetti into the air and declare today your spiritual birthday! The angels are celebrating in heaven all because of you!

"There will be more joy in heaven over one sinner who repents . . ."
~ Luke 15:7 NIV

(If you just gave your life to Jesus, please tell me at andrea@andrea stephens.com! I want to be in on the party too!)

The Bible tells us that when you become a child of God, a follower of Jesus, you get transferred from the kingdom of darkness to the kingdom of light—God's kingdom. And his king-

dom is full of righteousness (you now have right standing with God), peace (you have peace with God and a sense of security), and joy (deep delight as you live for him). Wow. You just get changed from the inside out!

You now have the blessings of eternal life, Jesus, and forgiveness. Well, buckle down, because here comes number four!

## 4. The Blessing of the Holy Spirit!

Okay, this is totally incredible. The minute you receive Jesus as your Lord and Savior, Father-God actually sends his Spirit to live inside you. He takes up residence in your body! (That truly makes you a divine diva.) The Spirit is living in you for a reason. A purpose. He has a job to do! He works in and through your life. It's his responsibility to (1) convict you of your sin (he lets you know you've sinned so you can ask for forgiveness), (2) remind you of the things you've learned about Jesus (this helps you live like Jesus lived), (3) guide you in God's ways (he keeps you on the right path), (4) comfort you when you're hurting (he's a great counselor), and (5) help you know how and what to pray (we sure need this). This is the role of the Spirit in your life. But check this out. He also fills you with power (the real kind).

---

A quick lesson: God the Father, God the Son, and God the Holy Spirit make up the Trinity. They are three in one. They are all deity, but they have different roles, different purposes, and different jobs to do.

# SPIRIT POWER: THE REAL DEAL

Don't let the fancy footwork, the impressive stunts, the illustrious illusions, or the sensational showmanship fool you. These Hollywood tricks only make Zena, Charlie's Angels, Lara Croft, Electra, and other megawomen *appear* powerful.

But it's all phony.

Well, guess what? **You've got the power.** Oh, no, not the Zena kind. You've got the real thing going on, B.A.B.E.! It's Holy Spirit power. We've looked at the Spirit's role in your life; now let me tell you about his supernatural power! See, the Spirit brings a different kind of power into your life. It's not about muscle strength or fast moves. It's a potent power provided by God's Spirit that makes you able to live for God, fight off your enemy (Satan), and control your natural human responses (like getting crazy mad or being super selfish). It's intensified, electrified, spiritfied! It's always at your fingertips 24/7. And it's there to be used for a purpose.

> You will receive **power** when the Holy Spirit has come upon you; and you shall be My witnesses.
>
> Acts 1:8 NASB

What is that purpose? Check out what the verse says. It's to be witnesses! Telling others about Jesus! Testifying to his saving grace!

*But I'm usually a chicken about opening my mouth to talk about Jesus!*

Well, forget that. Check this out:

> **Greater** is He who is **in you** than he who is in the world.
>
> 1 John 4:4 NASB

> For God has not given us a spirit of timidity [fear], but of **power**, love, and self-discipline [sound mind].
>
> 2 Timothy 1:7 NLT

The power in you is greater than the intimidation, teasing, mocking, or meanness that comes at you from others. So I'll say it again. **You've got the power!**

In fact, you're a **Secret Power Girl**. That's how *Brio* magazine editor (and my friend) Susie Shellenberger defines Holy Spirit–empowered chicas.

What is a Secret Power Girl? It's someone who has accepted Jesus Christ as her Lord, has consecrated her gifts for His use, is committed to pray and read the Bible, is dedicated to allowing the Holy Spirit to produce spiritual fruit in her life, and is in the process of discovering and developing her special power through her God-given gift.

Her strong relationship with Christ gives her confidence. And because she understands that God loves her no matter what, she loves and accepts herself. People are naturally attracted to a Secret Power Girl. They admire her confidence, and they are drawn to her genuineness. They want to be around her because she truly cares about others and is confident enough to reach out to them.

Is she perfect? No. But when she blows it, she seeks God's forgiveness and learns from her mistake. She's determined to become all that God dreams for her to be.*

You've got the power! Holy Spirit power! Cool, huh? Ever thought of yourself as God's secret powerhouse, always ready for God's assignment? Well, it's true. Allow it to affect your view of you! You are absolutely not a weak, powerless, wimpy wallflower who is worthless! You're a vessel of the living God, a container full of his Spirit!

*But wait, what if I don't feel any power?*

Spirit power isn't based on feelings, it's based on fact. And the fact is, if you have the Holy Spirit in you, you're a powerhouse. Question is, are you going to believe God's word to us in the Bible or your feelings?

> You are absolutely not a weak, powerless, wimpy wallflower who is worthless! You're a Spirit-filled powerhouse!

* You can find this info (check page 119) and other great stuff in Susie's book *Secret Power for Girls* published by Youth Specialties.

# Precious Fruit

The Holy Spirit is such a great blessing! Not only is he our helper, comforter, counselor, guide, teacher, prayer partner, and power source, he's also the one at work in our hearts, our innermost beings, building special qualities that make us shine from the inside out. These nine special qualities are called "fruit."

Imagine a grape arbor with the vine growing up and over a trellis. Growing out from that vine are branches, and hanging from the branches are delicious-looking bunches of grapes. Jesus used the vine to illustrate our relationship to him. He said, "Yes, I am the Vine; you are the branches. Whoever lives in me and I in him [and her] shall produce a large crop of fruit" (John 15:5 TLB). Since I live in California, this is a familiar scene for me. It constantly reminds me of Jesus's teaching.

Jesus lives in you through the Holy Spirit. When we, the branches, stay tight with Jesus, the Vine, we'll produce these special qualities, these fruit! So what kind of fruit are we talking about? The fruit you produce when you live in Jesus are **Love! Joy! Peace! Patience! Kindness! Goodness! Faithfulness! Gentleness! Self-Control!** When you produce these fruit, it proves that the Holy Spirit is living in you. They are the character and nature of Jesus living through you! They give you his peace when life is whirlwind crazy, his faithfulness to persevere when you want to give up, and so on. They let classmates and co-workers see you are different. Those around you will see Jesus in you and be drawn to him! They will be blessed by you! And this blesses your heavenly Father! This is the ultimate purpose of the fruit.

## Inside Edition:
# TRUE FRUIT WITH JOY WILLIAMS

Hands down, Joy Williams has one of the biggest and best smiles ever! It's genuine. It's real. It appears in an instant. It's a reflection of what's going on inside of this award-winning, internationally known contemporary Christian artist: joy!

Joy. It's much more than her name. It's the fruit of the Holy Spirit shining through her into a world that needs the light of Jesus. Joy to the world! It's declared in late December when we celebrate God sending Jesus into the world. Jesus *is* the joy that bubbles up and pours out of Joy Williams.

I've met and talked with Joy several times over the past few years. She even joined the *Brio* staff and hundreds of teen girls on our two-week *Brio* mission trip to Quito, Ecuador. She was put in all kinds of situations—tough, trying, out-of-her-comfort-zone kind of stuff. But it never left her. The smile, the joy, remained. We could see Jesus in her.

And that's one of her life goals.

Joy's song "Do They See Jesus in Me?" speaks of her desire to have people see Jesus in her, to recognize that she's a disciple of his, to have what she says and what she does communicate the Lord's love and his grace to those she comes into contact with. She wants the choices she makes to be a reflection of Jesus living in her.

I'm glad to say that I've seen Jesus in her. I've seen the Holy Spirit shining through her. I've seen an abundance of the fruit of joy in Joy! And it's a result of her relationship with the Lord. It's a result of her intentional choice to stay connected to the Vine. And it's reflected in her music. Music that honors God and keeps her listeners focused on doing the same!*

* Wanna know what's up with Joy? Check her at www.joywilliams .com!

If you become disconnected from the Vine, you'll minimize the Holy Spirit's work in your life—and you definitely won't produce his fruit. You'll suffer from spiritual malnutrition, and your fruit will fall off! You'll lose your love, your joy, your kindness toward others. You'll lose your power, your peace, and your patience. It's not attractive. You definitely won't feel blessed!

The Bible says when you disconnect you'll begin to see evil and ugly things cropping up in your life. These are the deeds or workings of your human nature, your flesh—things that are produced when you pull away from the Vine, when you toss your Bible on a shelf, drop out of youth group, quit showing up at Sunday school, turn the radio dial to a station that pumps out raunchy song lyrics, or get hooked on a TV show that trashes godly morals.

Flip your Bible open and read Galatians 5:16–23. Notice the fruit of the Spirit? Now zero in on the verses above them. List the nasty stuff in our flesh that surfaces when we aren't staying plugged in to Jesus:

Pretty ugly, huh?

Chances are, you're not going to murder anyone anytime soon, but raising your voice, slamming doors, arguing with your mom, being jealous of others, envying your girlfriend's family vacation, entertaining lustful thoughts, allowing other things to push God out of first-place position in your heart—these are things any of us could do at any time if we don't let the Spirit fully reign in us.

Even if we let him rule and reign half of the time, we still open ourselves to being easily tripped up. We end

**When you disconnect from Jesus, the Vine, you'll see wicked and ugly things cropping up in your life.**

up feeling pulled in both directions—going God's way, going our way. Life becomes even more of a battle, an inner battle. And indeed it is. Did you catch what verse 17 said? The flesh sets its desires against the Spirit and vice versa. They're like two forces boxing it out to win control over us.

Get out of the ring! Don't wait for the bell to ding or the round to end.

That's a battle you just don't want to be in! And it's a punching match to be avoided by not letting yourself get stuck between the flesh and the Spirit. (Take note that it's the **evil** flesh and the **Holy** Spirit.)

What's the key to keeping all this junk out of your life? Reread verse 16. The answer is right there. Record it here:

Walk by the Spirit! Follow the Spirit's lead. Stay plugged in to him. How? Through praying, reading the Bible (watch for the study tips coming up in section 4), meditating on Scripture, listening to Christian music, and guarding what you see and read. It's a choice you make every day! It's all about living intentionally! Then you and the Holy Spirit will produce unconditional love, unquenchable joy, unflappable peace, unshakable patience, unending kindness, uncontaminated goodness, undeniable faithfulness, unstirrable gentleness, and unrockable self-control. These inner qualities will make you even more babe-a-licious! (For the whole dish on the fruit of the Spirit, check out a copy of my book *True Beauty: The Inside Story*.)

*Incredible!* That's the word that describes the fruit of the Spirit. But hang on. Fruit is only half the story. This irreplaceable member of the Holy Trio brings yet another blessing into our lives. Gifts!

# GIFTS GALORE

I love my birthday. I adore Christmas. I get excited about Valentine's Day!

Can you guess why? I love gifts! If I see a beautifully wrapped box with a big bow on top, I'm drawn to its side. If a shiny gift bag with coordinating tissue paper is poised somewhere near me, I always sort of hope it's for me! But I don't tell anyone, because that's kind of tacky. Not a cool thing to confess. Yet since everyone likes getting gifts (come on, admit it—you're probably just like me), God has made it a point to give each of us at least one gift. This isn't just any gift; it's a spiritual gift. A spiritual blessing. It's unlike anything else you've ever received. It's unique. It's free and can't be earned. It's not a reward for good behavior. It's a gift. A gift that can never be taken away from you. It's yours for keeps. According to Peter Wagner, developer of a widely used spiritual gifts test called *Finding Your Spiritual Gifts*, a spiritual gift is a special ability God gives his children.*

# WHAT FLAVOR IS YOURS?

Have you ever gone into an ice cream shop like Baskin-Robbins and marveled at all the different flavors under the glass case? Mint chocolate chip. Jamaican almond fudge. Cookie dough. Pink

* Hey, pick up a copy of *Finding Your Spiritual Gifts: Wagner-Modified Houts Questionnaire* by C. Peter Wagner. He's a California dude.

bubble gum. Bobsled brownie. Winter white chocolate. Not to mention the wild and reckless sherbet! Sometimes it seems impossible to choose. It's a good thing they let you do a taste test. (Hey, if you didn't know about that, you've been missing out!) Just ask politely, and they give you a tiny spoon with your sample of choice. This helps you educate yourself on the flavors and know which ones are for you. After all, you have to know your stuff when it comes to ice cream.

Knowing your stuff is important when it comes to spiritual gifts too. You need to know what they are and test them out to see which ones are for you.

*Uh-oh.* You're thinking you don't know that much about spiritual gifts? You're not sure you remember ever **getting** a gift? You don't even know what they are or what yours might be?

If you lived in Bible times, you'd be in big trouble. Paul had some choice things to say to those who got this spiritual gift stuff all wrong. Don't be brainless! Don't be oblivious! Don't be misinformed! That's pretty much what Paul said to the members of the church in Corinth when he said, "Now about spiritual gifts, brothers [and sisters], I do not want you to be ignorant" (1 Corinthians 12:1 NIV). I'm thrilled they recorded that in the Bible, because Paul would say the same thing to us today! He would want us to know and understand the gifts the Holy Spirit blesses us with (and yep, just like with the fruit, these gifts make us a blessing to others and the Lord too).

So grab your Bible and your favorite pen, and let's get started. Be an informed B.A.B.E.!

# JUST THE FACTS, PLEASE

Let's dig into this gift stuff, because it's stuff you've gotta know! It's stuff that supports the fact that you're blessed. It's stuff that will boost the way you see yourself and expand your vision of all the ways you can serve Jesus. It will increase your awareness of what God has planned for your life! So set your eyes on the following verses, fill in the blanks, and get ready to discover more about who you are in Christ and how God has equipped you to become all you can be for him!

### John 3:5–6; John 14:16–17

When you're _____ of the Spirit (when you invite Jesus into your life to be your Lord and Savior), he comes to live on the _____ of you. This is your spiritual birthday, and you get spiritual gifts!

### 1 Corinthians 12:12–24

All gifts are equally important to assist us in fulfilling our _____ in the body of _____. We need each other!

### Romans 12:3–8

We have different gifts and different functions, but we're all an important part of the _____ of Christ.

Jot down the seven gifts.

### Ephesians 4:11–13

God has given the body of Christ these gifts to _____ his people (the saints) for the work of _____ so that the body of Christ will be built _____ so that we'll reach _____ in the faith and in _____ of the Son of God and become ____ _____!

List the five gifts.

### 1 Corinthians 12:4–11

There are _____ kinds of gifts but the same _____ (verse 4).

Gifts are given to benefit _____ _____ (verse 7).

All of these are the work of one and the same _____, and he gives gifts to each one, just as he _____ (verse 11).

Jot down the nine gifts.

(Did you notice: healing, miracles, and faith deal with **actions**; tongues, interpretation, and prophecy relate to **words**; discernment, wisdom, and knowledge require a special knowing or insightful **thoughts**. God wants to invade our whole person.)

### 1 Corinthians 12:28

List the two gifts mentioned here that aren't listed in the other 1 Corinthians verses.

Finished? Test yourself based on what your brain just lapped up!

True or false?

\_\_\_ It's possible to have a spiritual gift and not be aware of it.

\_\_\_ You receive your spiritual gift when you become a mature believer.

\_\_\_ It's okay to pray for a certain gift.

\_\_\_ The Holy Spirit dishes out the gifts.

\_\_\_ You're the one who decides what gift you're given.

\_\_\_ Your gifts aren't about you. They're there for you to help and benefit your brothers and sisters in Christ and the growth of the church (yep, serving God means serving others). This is the goal of the Spirit giving us gifts!

\_\_\_ It's totally cool to brag about your gifts. After all, they're from God.

\_\_\_ Every believer has at least one gift.

\_\_\_ The Holy Spirit gives you gifts when he comes into your life—at the time of your spiritual birth.

And that's not all . . .

The gifts spoken of in the Bible don't necessarily compose an all-inclusive list. God is God! He can gift a person with whatever he wants whenever he wants.

Because these are spiritual gifts, they're primarily used for God-related situations. (A gift of healing may very well work on a sick person but not on a broken CD player. *Comprende?*)

The Spirit hands out gifts as God wills, but we need to develop them by using them. It's just like developing your muscles.

Gifts are to be used here and now, on earth. They won't be needed in heaven.

One gift isn't better or more important than another. They're equally needed.

No one has **all** the gifts (well, Jesus did, but hey, he was totally human *and* totally God).

The Holy Spirit can give you different gifts or more gifts throughout your life so that your gifts match up with the assignment God has for you. That's right. Your gifts allow you to fill a specific role in your church, your community, your family, or the world. Sometimes when you change churches or move to a different city or neighborhood or go to a new school, God will give you a new gift or just add to the one you already have because there's a need in that place for someone with that gift.

Different people have different gifts. Beware of **comparing** or becoming frustrated with someone who doesn't see or do things your way. Enjoy and appreciate the gifts God has given you—comparing ruins that! Enjoy what the Lord has given others by appreciating their gifts and the unique way they use them.

# Defining Moments

Okay, so you've identified the gifts and found out a few facts, and there's no chance of you falling into the unaware or ignorant category. Whew! Now it's time to define these delightful gifts.

As you digest these definitions, keep a careful eye on which ones you think might be describing you! This will get you primed and pumped up for the test that's headed your way just a few pages from now. Remember, you have a minimum of one gift, but you may discover two or three gifts that you've seen at work in your life.

## The Gifts in Romans

**Proclamation/Prophecy:** Hearing a special "right now" message from God and speaking to his people as a whole or to an individual person.

**Serving:** Recognizing jobs that need to be done and finding a way to complete them.

**Teaching:** Communicating biblical information (by word and deed) so others can understand and grow in their knowledge of the Lord.

**Encouragement/Exhortation:** Speaking a word of encouragement or advice that often inspires the faith of others.

**Giving:** Cheerfully and generously sharing what you have with others.

**Leading:** Catching God's vision, setting goals, and influencing others to help reach them.

**Mercy:** Genuinely feeling what others are feeling, then being sympathetic, comforting, and kind toward them.

## The Gifts in 1 Corinthians

**Wisdom:** Using Holy Spirit–given insight to give biblical wisdom right when it's needed.

**Knowledge:** Discovering, understanding, and clarifying information to help God's people.

**Faith:** Having unquenchable trust and confidence about God's plan and purposes.

**Healing:** Laying hands on sick people, praying for them, and seeing God cure them.

**Miracles:** Serving as the human instrument that receives God's power to perform powerful acts.

**Discernment:** Knowing if a person's spirit or motivation is of God or of Satan.

**Speaking in Spiritual Language:** Receiving and delivering a message from God through a divine language (tongues) you've never learned. Also used in private prayer.

**Interpreting Spiritual Language:** Receiving from God the translation of a message given in spiritual language (tongues).

**Helps:** Working behind the scenes to assist others in fulfilling their ministry.

**Administration:** Creating a practical plan and organizing others to complete it.

**Prophecy:** Already defined.

### The Gifts in Ephesians

**Apostle:** Creating new situations to formally and purposefully gather believers together (a new church, Bible study, or youth group).

**Evangelist:** Sharing the Good News of Jesus and winning nonbelievers to Christ.

**Pastor/Shepherd:** Providing the care and spiritual feeding of God's people.

**Prophet:** Already defined.

**Teacher:** Already defined.

### A Few More Gifts Found Other Places in Scripture

**Celibacy:** Remaining single and sexually abstinent for purposes of serving God (1 Corinthians 7:7–8).

**Hospitality:** Opening your home and heart to those who need food or lodging. The ability to make others feel welcome (1 Peter 4:9).

**Intercession:** Praying on behalf of others, standing in the gap between them and God, holding them up to heaven until the prayer is answered (Colossians 1:9).

# LIGHTS, camera, action

Find out if you're grasping the definitions of the gifts. Do the match-up thing as a way of testing your ability to recognize some of the gifts in action! Draw a line from the gift to the girl who's got it!

| Gift | See It for Yourself |
|------|---------------------|
| Giving | Kim pulled together a team of students and created a plan for getting more classmates to attend See You at the Pole. |
| Administration | As Sierra's small group was closing in prayer, the Holy Spirit showed her what her friend could do to get along better with his parents. |
| Faith | Katie was pumped about having her soccer coach over for dinner. Cooking, decorating, and making it special was so fun to her. |
| Hospitality | Jamie's friends were dogging on the new girl at school, when Jamie heard in her head, "The way you judge others is the way the Lord will judge you," and felt the urge to tell them immediately. |
| Wisdom | Brittnee saw a customer spill a steaming hot latte on her hand. She rushed over and prayed, and the pain was instantly gone. |
| Healing | Meg overheard Lori say she couldn't afford to go on the youth group retreat, so she used her own money to pay Lori's way. |
| Mercy | When Crystal's grandmother died, Angie just had to go over to Crystal's to comfort her. |
| Prophecy | Even though Christa's brother thought she was naïve for believing God would provide the cash for her mission trip, Christa had total confidence in God. |

How did you do? In reverse order, here are the gifts and the girls who matched them. Prophecy: Jamie; Mercy: Angie; Healing: Brittnee; Wisdom: Sierra; Hospitality: Katie; Faith: Christa; Administration: Kim; Giving: Meg.

## In Her Own Words . . .

God created His people with so many different talents. We're each a unique member of the body of Christ. But if we're too busy trying to be someone else, then we can miss out on what God called us to do. We'll never fulfill His plan for our lives. We need to focus on what He created us to be, not on what others say or think about us.*

~ Stacy Orrico

*Find out more of what's in Stacy Orrico's head and heart in her book *Genuine*. Check out this quote on page 61.

129

# WHAT'S IN YOUR GIFT BOX?

Are you starting to sense what's in your spiritual gift box? Let's lift the box lid a bit farther. These tips will help you see what's inside.

**Gifts in action!** Study the use of the gifts in the Bible to see if they describe you and if God has used you in the same way. For example, in Acts 6:1–7, the disciples used the gift of administration to delegate the church work so that all people would be served. Mary Magdalene had the gift of giving and financially supported Jesus's ministry (Luke 8:2–3).

**Try them on!** When it comes to clothes, you take an armful into the dressing room, slip them on, and check yourself out. Is it the right fit? Does it reflect your style and personality? Are you comfortable in it? Do the same with the spiritual gifts. Try them on. Step up to the vice-president role in a club (leadership), or volunteer to stuff envelopes for a local charity event (helps). Try being a chaplain in Fellowship of Christian Athletes (pastor/shepherd) or writing uplifting emails to your friends (exhortation/encouragement). Experimenting with different gifts will help you pinpoint what your individual gifts are. Remember, true gifts are backed up with godly passion and purpose.

**Talk it out!** Run it by people who know you really, really well—inside and out. Your parents, stepparents, grandparents, bros and sisses, closest gal pals, youth pastors, Sunday school teachers, or coaches are all good options. Ask them which gifts they see in you.

**Pay attention!** You know what you have is a gift when you excel at it, when it ignites your passion. For instance, God asks all of us to tell others about Jesus (evangelism), but if you're compelled to do it, it's a gift! Not to say that if you're compelled to eat, you have the gift of munch! You get my point, right?

# Taking Stock of Your Spiritual Gifts

Okay, B.A.B.E., now that you're up to the minute on spiritual gifts, are you ready to discover which ones the Holy Spirit has blessed *you* with?

Taking this test is going to be fun. But before you bust out of the starting gate, take time to pray. Ask the Lord to make your gift(s) clear to you. Pray for spiritual insight as you thoughtfully read and consider which gifts are yours. As you're taking the test, go with your initial, gut-level reaction. Avoid second-guessing.

**Directions**: Under each letter, place a Y for "Yes" by the statements that describe you. Place an N for "No" by those that don't. Oh, and one suggestion: this will take a while, so you might want to go get a handful of pretzels and grab another Gatorade!

## A

_____ I like others to know they can depend on me.

_____ Sometimes I say yes too quickly and get overcommitted.

_____ I can easily see what tasks/jobs need done, and I do them even if it means being inconvenienced.

_____ I love hanging with people while working on a project.

_____ I don't understand why others don't help out when there's an obvious need.

_____ I do more than others ask me to do.

_____ Big job, little job—I just love helping out.

## B

_____ If someone is way off base about something, I can gently correct him or her if necessary.

_____ My friends confide in me and come to me for advice.

_____ I notice when people are emotionally upset, and I want to comfort them.

_____ When I see people struggling with an issue, I often show them what the Bible says about it.

_____ I can see potential in others and support them to be all they can be.

_____ I'm usually optimistic and in a good mood.

_____ Okay, I admit it. Sometimes I'm too quick to open my mouth and offer solutions before I know the whole story.

## C

_____ I believe that what the Bible says is more important than my personal opinion.

_____ My girlfriends have told me they think I'm insightful.

_____ As I listen to a person's problems, I quickly pray for the Lord to give me the right words to say to them.

_____ When others see a problem as being complex, I can usually see a simple solution.

_____ I can apply God's Word to everyday situations.

_____ Many people have commented that I'm mature for my age.

## D

_____ I wish there were Bible studies on every school campus, and I would love to start one wherever I could.

_____ I would have no problem going to the school board to present a plan to start FCA (Fellowship of Christian Athletes) on my school campus.

_____ If I heard about a small group Bible study that was about to disband, I would join just to keep it together.

_____ I eventually get restless with established groups and want to move on to new things.

_____ If God urged me to start a church, I would be jazzed about it.

_____ When it comes to spiritually related issues, others seem to respect me as someone who is well versed.

## E

_____ I love tackling a big project and organizing the how-tos.

_____ Working on projects can be more fun than just hanging with my friends.

_____ I enjoy taking on new tasks.

_____ I'm a goal setter and list maker.

_____ Sometimes I make plans and pull together the people to make them happen.

_____ I get uptight when things aren't done my way.

_____ I get my head so into successfully finishing a project that I often forget to encourage and thank others.

_____ I don't try to accomplish goals all by myself. I share the load.

_____ When other people's gifts and talents are evident, I like to plug them in to jobs that will satisfy them.

_____ Making important decisions doesn't scare me.

## F

_____ I absolutely believe that God's Word is the truth and is the key to everything.

_____ I'm not afraid to remind my friends of God's will and what will happen if they choose to blow it off.

_____ I truly sense the Holy Spirit's power and presence with me when I'm speaking in front of a crowd.

_____ I get pumped to defend my faith. Bring it on!

_____ Sometimes I'm too blunt and can hurt others' feelings.

_____ When I sense something is going to happen, I'm usually right.

## G

_____ The idea of anyone going to hell makes me shudder.

_____ It's sorta adventurous for me to see if I can bring a conversation around to God.

_____ I'm always ready to tell others about Jesus.

_____ I get sad thinking about classmates who don't know Jesus.

_____ I've brought people to saving faith in Christ.

_____ I believe telling others about God's love and Jesus's death on the cross for their sake is more important than anything.

_____ I like being with nonbelievers, with hopes of telling them about my relationship with Jesus.

## H

_____ I'm willing to give up my own time for those I'm close to.

_____ My girlfriends say I tend to mother them.

_____ I'm discipling one or more younger girls to help them grow in their faith.

_____ I'm compelled to get a friend back on track with God.

_____ Sometimes I like it when others need me or are dependent on me.

_____ I feel genuinely distraught when a friend walks away from God.

_____ I feel fulfilled when I help others grow in their relationship with Jesus.

_____ I try to steer others away from wrong influences that could negatively affect their walk with God and their witness for Jesus.

_____ I'm so grateful when God uses me to bring someone back to him.

## I

_____ I can totally lose myself in Bible study.

_____ God's Word fascinates me, and I want others to feel the same.

_____ When I learn something new about the Bible, I have to share it.

_____ Researching a Bible passage and looking for answers is fun to me.

_____ Because I have studied, I'm pretty good at answering questions about the Bible.

_____ I have an ability to help others clearly understand God's Word.

_____ Occasionally I get prideful about knowing more than others.

_____ Others say I explain the Bible in ways that help them learn.

_____ I think object lessons rock.

## J

_____ I have a passionate belief that God will do what he says he'll do.

_____ I can calmly wait for God to answer prayer.

_____ I'm convinced that God is faithful and that what he leads me to do will be successful.

_____ I'm not discouraged by others' doubt, but I can get down when they won't trust God.

_____ Lots of people come to me for assurance.

_____ I wish everyone had unquenchable confidence in God's love for us.

_____ I know the Lord will work on my behalf so I can do what he calls me to do.

## K

_____ I get jazzed about discovering new stuff about God.

_____ Others say that what I share touches and changes them.

_____ I've been accused of "having all the answers."

_____ When I'm studying or praying, thoughts come into my mind that seem to be directly from God.

_____ I've sensed a "knowing" from God when others haven't.

_____ I thrive on gaining information and insight about God, his words, his ways.

### L

_____ Doing the small jobs is satisfying to me—stuffing envelopes, calling lists, cleaning out the church/ youth van.

_____ I enjoy relieving another person of the typical little tasks so he or she can do something else.

_____ I get stressed being up in front of people.

_____ I tend to put others' needs first and often neglect my own needs.

_____ I admit that I occasionally feel used.

_____ There's no way I would run for class president.

_____ Who gets the credit? I don't want it or need it.

_____ If I had a ton on my plate, I would have a hard time distributing jobs to others.

_____ I'm the first to volunteer to help the youth pastor/ children's director.

### M

_____ People trust me to be honest and do the right thing.

_____ I thrive on figuring out the steps needed to reach a goal.

_____ I'm kind of like a pied piper— people follow my lead.

_____ I like teamwork and am okay with asking others to help me accomplish a task for the church/Lord.

_____ I'm comfortable delegating work to others.

_____ Sometimes I get single focused and forget to ask others' opinions and ideas.

_____ If no one will step up to the plate, I'll take over.

### N

_____ I get frustrated when I pray but don't see change.

_____ I've seen God's power heal someone through my prayers said in Jesus's name.

_____ When God gets glory for his power, I'm thrilled.

_____ My faith has helped heal others.

_____ I like praying for people who have physical illnesses.

_____ Those who are sick ask me to pray for them.

_____ I care about the physical, emotional, mental, and spiritual health of others.

## O

_____ I think it's fun to give others anonymous gifts.

_____ I'm willing to do what's necessary to see God's work get done (money/time).

_____ Yes, sign me up to raise money to be a Compassion International child sponsor.

_____ I enjoy coming up with ways to raise money.

_____ Fund-raisers are fun to me.

_____ I think all money is really God's, and he leads me as to how to use it.

_____ I would rather give my babysitting bucks to a good cause than buy myself a new outfit.

_____ The Bible says to give God 10 percent, but I want to give more.

_____ I enjoy giving money to those in financial need, and I don't expect anything in return.

_____ When God blesses me with extra money, I start praying about who he wants me to bless.

## P

_____ I've seen God use me to do supernatural things.

_____ My prayers are full of faith.

_____ If I know God has directed me to do something, I'll do it even if it sounds crazy to others.

_____ I give God credit for his actions, and I know they're not mere coincidences.

_____ When I pray, God often makes the impossible possible.

_____ I've done things beyond my human ability.

## Q

_____ I can strongly sense right from wrong (even when others can't).

_____ I know that just because something is supernatural doesn't mean it's of God.

_____ I usually know when others are lying and being fake.

_____ Others have told me I have sound spiritual judgment.

_____ I can tell whether a youth pastor or speaker is anointed by God.

_____ I easily see situations from God's perspective.

## R

_____ I'm very welcoming, even to those I don't know very well.

_____ People say I make them feel comfortable.

_____ I like volunteering to have people over to my house.

_____ Need snacks? I'll bring some.

_____ If a traveling youth choir were performing at my church, I would want a bunch of them to stay at my house.

_____ I choose to show God's love, not just entertain.

_____ My favorite job is being a greeter.

## S

_____ I've spoken in a spiritual language that's a tongue I never learned.

_____ I don't understand what I'm saying when I use my spiritual language.

_____ During prayer, when I find myself at a loss for words, I use my spiritual language.

_____ The Holy Spirit has used me to deliver a message out loud at church/youth service in a spiritual language.

_____ Others have interpreted my message given in tongues.

_____ I've interpreted messages that others have given in tongues.

## T

_____ I'm influenced more by my emotions than by thoughts.

_____ I recognize it when others are hurting in some way.

_____ When I see someone in crisis, I can imagine myself in his or her situation.

_____ When I overhear someone being criticized, I don't like it.

_____ Others say I'm compassionate and good at cheering them up.

_____ I find myself being attracted to those who are needy.

_____ I have no problem going to hospitals or nursing homes to visit patients.

_____ When other kids at school are rejected, I'm willing to be their friend.

## U

_____ I'm often drawn into prayer, sometimes for long periods of time.

_____ I enjoy praying for others.

_____ If there's a problem, I'm the first to say, "Let's pray."

_____ People ask me to pray for them.

_____ I have prayer categories (family, friends, school, unsaved, sick).

_____ Since prayer is my thing, I stick with it.

_____ I believe prayer is the most important role of Christians.

_____ I eventually see my prayers answered.

**V**

_____ I'm cool with the idea of being single and available for God's work.

_____ I choose not to become romantically involved with guys.

_____ God is my companion (and confidant).

_____ I sometimes struggle with loneliness.

_____ I can get frustrated when my friends go crazy over a guy and just drop their girlfriends.

_____ If God called me to move by myself to a foreign country, I wouldn't panic over the possibility of never meeting "marriage material" there.

**DON'T EVEN THINK ABOUT PEEKING AT THE NEXT SECTION UNTIL YOU HAVE COMPLETED THE CHECKLIST!**

Note: There are many different types of spiritual gifts tests and assessments available. You can test your brains away! Just don't forget that the best way to confirm your gifts is to get out there and try them! Here are a few sites you might like: Gifted2Serve—go to www.buildingchurch.net; Spiritual Gifts Analysis—go to www .churchgrowth.org. Two sites that key in on a partial list of gifts are www.eleventalents.com and www.elmertowns.com. Have fun!

# Dancing in the Rain

Done? Kinda long, huh? But worth it, I promise!

Ready to see what gifts the heavenly Father has showered down on you? Ready to delight in them and maybe even do a little dance? Here we go!

Glance back over your answers. Some letters will have many Y's, and others will have few. Circle three or four letters that have the most Y's. These will be the ones whose descriptions fit you best.

Next, the funnest part. (That's not a word, so why do people use it all the time?)

Go back through the test and write the name of the gift next to the corresponding letter. Here they are:

A=Service

B=Encouragement

C=Wisdom

D=Apostle

E=Administration

F=Proclamation/
Prophecy

G=Evangelism

H=Pastor/Shepherd

I=Teaching

J=Faith

K=Knowledge

L=Helps

M=Leading

N=Healing

O=Giving

P=Miracles

Q=Discernment

R=Hospitality

S=Spiritual Language/
Interpretation

T=Mercy

U=Intercession

V=Celibacy

Go back to check out the letters you circled. Are you surprised? Or did you already have a strong hunch what your gift(s) might be? Jot them down:

I have been blessed with:

Just for kicks, identify which gifts aren't yours by looking at the N's. Check the corresponding gift(s).

I am definitely not gifted with:

Now that you have a strong idea of your perfect presents from God, what are you going to do with what you know? See, the reason I've given you so much information about spiritual gifts is because they play a huge part in knowing how God may use you to make a difference in his name, even now, as a teen! They'll help you see what plans and purposes he has for your life, how you're eternally significant. (Yep! That's the next section of this book.) Remember, your gifts aren't for you. They're to be used to bless others; to build up the body of Christ, the church, the youth group; and to show God's radical, unconditional love in every encounter you have! You're blessed so you can be a blessing. And ultimately who gets most blessed? God does! You, my friend, have an incredible way of putting a smile on his face.

Okay, for what type of ministries or activities could you use your spiritual gift(s)?

For example, leadership might be your thing. You would be right at home heading up the youth room redecorating project or motivating others to participate in the 30 Hour Famine (www.30hourfamine.org).

Let's say encouragement ranks high. Try speaking kindly to the outcast or shy girls at school or sending notes with uplifting Scriptures to four people who need a shot of support (don't forget your church staff and church missionaries).

If healing landed in your top four, why not designate a time and place after church or at school when you could pray over students with physical illnesses?

Get it? Good. Now get going.

Brainstorm, think outside the box, and talk it over with family and friends!

Here are a few more ideas some of my teen friends came up with. They're general, but you can apply them to fit your gift:

Volunteer a few hours a week in the church office, help out in the nursery, learn PowerPoint so you can add visuals to sermons or praise time, coordinate the cleanup for the next youth group event, organize a car wash for a friend's mission trip, offer to babysit for free, start a youth magalog, or develop a prayer chain.

Good ideas, huh? The ways God can use you and your gifts are endless!

Okay, B.A.B.E., you've got the skinny on the spiritual gifts. You now have the official who, what, where, when, and why on the Holy Spirit's blessings. We're talking power, fruit, and gifts. The more you work with him, the Holy Spirit will help you become all God has created you to be. God doesn't play favorites. You're as blessed as the next chick. You've got the same potential as that person you've been envious of, because **you**, girl, are blessed!

I've now shared my top four spiritual blessings: Jesus, forgiveness, eternal life, and the Holy Spirit. Yes, there are many more, like grace and mercy. Do you have a few in mind that are your favorites? Add them here:

# Naturally You!

Okay, so we've talked a lot about spiritual blessings and gifts. But there are some other blessings we should take a look at too. Blessings you've had from the moment you were born.

Your life began at the moment of conception. In those first few moments of your life, while you were still a small group of cells, God was arranging your DNA. He carefully and intentionally included the needed ingredients that would cause you to develop certain natural abilities. Like spiritual gifts, these abilities come from God, but they were there at your first birth! You were literally born with them!

God gives us these natural abilities as he sees fit. We don't all get the same ones or the same amount. We get what God wants us to have. And they go along with the purpose he has for our lives. Sometimes we don't acknowledge the things we enjoy and are good at as being from God, but they are. God uses our natural abilities to fulfill the special jobs he has for us to do. And we can find enjoyment and contentment in that!

God has quite a selection of natural abilities he might have blessed you with. Let's look at some of them. Ready?

**Musical abilities**, like singing, songwriting, or playing an instrument (even a tambourine). Maybe you'll have all three, like artists Bethany Dillion, Nicole Nordeman, and Jennifer Knapp!

**Artistic abilities**, like drawing, fashion design, graphic arts, or decorating. Crafts, woodworking, painting, scrapbooking, and even fancy napkin folding count as your artistic flare shining through!

**Domestic abilities**, like baking, cooking, housecleaning, laundry, gardening, or sewing. Becca, one of our youth group girls, began sewing drawstring purses and selling them to raise money for a mission trip. I sewed a lot as a teen. I made blouses, skirts, prom dresses, and even a bathing suit. (Unfortunately, the fabric I selected for my tankini expanded in the water! Not good, believe me!)

**Academic abilities**, like learning, studying, writing essays, or scoring well on SATs. Carey, one of the *Brio* Girl finalists, loves to write. She entered the *Guideposts* Young Writers Contest and came in third in the nation. Her article, printed in the magazine, was read by thousands.

**Athletic abilities**, like basketball, baseball, volleyball, soccer, swimming, tennis, track—all the sports. And let's not leave out weight lifting, ice skating, Rollerblading, and dancing! My neighbor was a national roller-skating champion, and now her fifteen-year-old daughter is competing!

I have to admit that God didn't put "athlete" on my natural abilities list. I'm not athletically blessed, I'm athletically challenged! When I was growing up, all the neighborhood kids gathered in the vacant lot down the street after dinner for our nightly game of kickball. What position did I play? Scorekeeper! Then, in fourth grade, I had my first encounter with a softball. I was walking across the playground at recess—totally minding my own business—when a wayward ball came flying right at me, struck the corner of my horn-rimmed glasses, and sent them sailing! Blood trickled down my temple as I decided I never again wanted to come in contact with a softball.

As a freshman in high school, I decided to try a sport that didn't involve a ball. My girlfriend, who was a totally buff B.A.B.E., talked me into going out for track with her. After three days of practice, I could barely walk. I had horrible shin splints and practically had to crawl on my hands and knees up the stairs between classes. I quit. (I know, you're shocked, aren't you?)

A few years later, I was in the Junior Miss Scholarship Program, which counts physical fitness as a percentage of the overall score. Well, there I was on stage, right in front of the judges, trying to complete my routine with ten push-ups. I struggled through seven and eight, then made it to nine but never came up for the last one. I didn't win. Go figure.

In college I tried coed volleyball. This guy served the ball right to me. I closed my eyes (like I always do when I see a ball flying at me) and hit the ball as hard as I could. I opened my eyes and looked across the net to see where I had skillfully sent the ball, but everyone was looking at me! There wasn't a ball in sight. Three seconds later, the ball came straight down and hit me on the top of my head. Now I only play sports where I'm behind the ball. I golf and I bowl. End of story!

What are your natural abilities? What have you tried, liked, and done well?

God made us good at **different** things, but he made us **all** to be good at **something**! Look for your natural abilities. They may not be among the ones listed here, but you have natural talents you can develop by reading up on them, taking lessons, joining a team, and putting them into use. Practice makes perfect!

When you seriously excel at your abilities, you'll like the results!

1. You'll be more effective in ministry.
2. You'll increase the ways God can use you.
3. You'll enjoy life even more.
4. Your confidence will be pumped up to a new level.

Kristy Starling put in lots of hours at voice lessons and running through songs. As her singing got better and better, she gained confidence in her ability. So much so that she entered the NBC *Today* Show's "Today's Superstar" and took second place! She was offered a recording contract with Warner Brothers Records, Christian Music Division, releasing her first CD only a few weeks later.

Excelling at your talents will help you to feel okay about the areas in which you're not especially talented. Of course you can't be good at everything. No one is. Yet having a few things you *are* good at evens the playing field.

Developing your natural abilities is up to you. God provided them, but you must put in the time and effort to develop them. If you think it's not a big deal, eventually that may become your general MO toward life—it's not a big deal. What a downer! Don't go there. Be the best you that you can be by developing and using all God has given you! What a blessing your gifts will be to you and the Lord!

**What do you get when you mix your spiritual gifts with your natural abilities? A very cool you!**

# Kaleidoscope Blessings

Did you notice from the opinion poll at the opening of this section that some girls define blessings based on being in the right place at the right time, being lucky, having life go your way, or being in a good mood? But these are situations that can come and go. Based on that definition, sometimes you'd be blessed, sometimes not.

And a whole lotta girls think they're *not* blessed because raunchy stuff happens. They flunk a test, fight with their parents, get sick, get abused in some way, get rejected by peers. This list is endless. Yes, life can be unfair. Yes, rotten things happen. That's the way life is sometimes, even for God's kids. Just because you've given your life to Jesus doesn't mean you're free and clear of the tough stuff, that life won't get hard. In fact, Jesus said it would:

> Here on earth you will have
> many trials and sorrows.
> But take heart, because I
> have overcome the world.
>
> John 16:33 NLT

Sometimes you have to go through tough times. I know, I've been there. There are two very tough experiences that stand out in my mind. First, the year I was in the Miss Oklahoma Pageant was one of diligent studying, perfecting my performance on classical guitar, nailing down my knowledge and opinions of current events, and polishing my poise. During the pageant I noticed there was a girl who excelled at her talent but walked like a cow. Watching her come down the stairs on stage was painful. So I pulled her aside and taught her how to do it correctly (I was teaching in a modeling school at this point). Guess what? She won! I didn't get it. I couldn't understand God's plan. I was tempted to be mad at myself that I'd helped her. I couldn't see the plan at the time, but two months later I was offered the contract with Wilhelmina Models, Inc., in New York City. Then two years after that, when I returned from New York to see what else God wanted to do in my life, the scholarship money I earned in the pageant (I won preliminary swimsuit and was a runner-up) paid my tuition to Bible school. God had it all under control!

Second, for many years I struggled to get pregnant. I had

seven surgeries, used powerful fertility drugs, went to hundreds of doctor appointments, and even tried unusual treatments like drinking green barley juice and taking organic herbs. I just wanted to have a baby, *my* baby. But nothing ever worked. Everything was unsuccessful, and I remain childless. I've finally given away the frilly dresses with matching hats and the hand-knit booties I've saved for years. Yes, it hurts. No, I don't understand it. But no, I'm not mad at God!

So many things will happen in your life that you won't understand. But you and I have to choose to continue to hang on to God's hand and keep loving him and trusting him even when we don't get answers to our questions, when heaven seems silent.

> Trust in the LORD with all your heart
> and lean not on your own understanding;
> in all your ways acknowledge him,
> and he will make your paths straight.
>
> Proverbs 3:5 NIV

This is one of my life verses. Maybe it will be one of yours. We each need the reminder to totally trust God with our whole heart, not just hoping he can pull us through a situation, but knowing he can. The verse clearly states *not* to try to figure it all out. So what are you supposed to do instead? Stay focused on God and your spiritual blessings. Be watching for him. Keep him in first place in your heart. Keep reading the Bible. God will be faithful to lead you.

In the middle of tough times, we must remember that God is still almighty God. He's an expert at making everything bad work out for good.

> And we know that in all things God works for the good of those who love him.
>
> Romans 8:28 NIV

Do you love the Lord? Do you live for him? He'll work things out!

As a kid, I used to love looking into a long **kaleidoscope**, slowly turning the end piece, creating colorful patterns. I believe that God guides us through twists and turns that arrange the pieces of our lives into patterns that create beautiful pictures. God does that with our lives. That's another blessing. We can trust our lives in his hands.

And yes, I'm saying we can be blessed in the midst of a tough time, and we can even get to the point that we consider a tough time a blessing because of the things you are learning.

Have you already experienced a tough or painful situation? Jot it down:

Add the blessings you received in the midst of the situation and those you can see now looking back on it:

Here's a verse that helps us through the rough spots.

> In everything give thanks; for this is God's will for you in Christ Jesus.
>
> 1 Thessalonians 5:18 NASB

Notice that it says "*in* everything" we are to give thanks. Apparently, it's possible to have a thankful attitude even when everything seems to tilt, even when life throws you a curveball or takes an unexpected turn. That's thanks*living*! Yet notice something else. The verse doesn't say "*for* everything" give thanks. See the difference? You won't always be grateful for the situation itself; however, in the midst of the situation, you can find things to be grateful for, blessings that are tucked inside! You can make the choice to rejoice!

Psalm 118:24 says, "This is the day the LORD has made; let us rejoice and be glad in it" (NIV). It's a choice! Say this phrase out loud, emphasizing each word in bold.

**I** will rejoice and be glad.
I **will** rejoice and be glad.
I will **rejoice** and be glad.
I will rejoice and be **glad**.

Kinda fun, huh? See how putting the punch on different words adds new meaning? Yet bottom line, **it all adds up to a decision you make**. Will you rejoice or will you not? Will you be glad or grumpy? Cheerful or crabby? Your attitude will affect your life. Your attitude will affect whether you view happenings in your life as blessings or bummers. Your attitude will affect your relationships with others (people like hanging with grateful girls). Every day before your ten toes hit the floor, will you be grateful for the new day the Lord has given you? Will you rejoice? Will you say thanks?

Easy? No. Possible and worth it? Yes!

## Strike Three, You're Out:
# THE ALESE COCO STORY

Alese Coco, a high school senior, was busy living life, making graduation plans, applying at colleges, and hanging out at Starbucks with friends. One Friday night after she returned home from a football game, she reached up to scratch her neck and felt a lump. She showed it to her parents, who took her to the emergency room immediately.

A few days later, the results of a needle biopsy were revealed.

Cancer.

Strike one!

On November 16, 2001, Alese Coco was diagnosed with Hodgkin's Lymphoma, cancer of the lymphatic system. A quick biology lesson: The lymph system is a network of vessels with the highly important job of filtering dangerous wastes, infections, and cancers from the body. When it doesn't function properly, those waste products build up and are overtaken, causing various illnesses like cancer.

"*Cancer* is a scary word. Anytime someone says cancer, you automatically think of death. For the first few days, I was really scared, and then I realized that if it's me or cancer, the score had to be in my favor, because I was still here."

Treatment began with six months of a chemotherapy protocol called ABVD (four powerful drugs: Adriamycin, bleomycin, vincristine, and dacarbazine). Targeting cancer cells, the potent drugs surged through Alese's system in a search-and-destroy mode. This left her feeling extremely sick and emotionally drained.

As the initial shock of the "C word" wore off, Alese and her parents had long talks about God and his sovereignty (absolute control). This led to an increase of Alese's faith. "There were so many people praying for me, and I truly felt God's hand in my life and knew he had a plan."

Several months later, Alese was declared cancer free. The treatment had been successful.

This is when I met Alese at Hume Lake Christian Conference Center, where I was speaking at the high school camp. She bravely stood before seven hundred peers, telling her story, which ended with the removal of her wig.

To her, the stubs of blond hair growing on her head were a sign of victory.

The score was Alese 1, cancer 0.

After graduation, Alese enrolled at El Camino Junior College. Except for the routine checkups every three months, cancer was far from her mind. She had some catching up to do, but life was pretty much back to normal.

Then came strike two.

"No one, including my doctors, my parents, or me, thought this disease would return. After the lump initially resurfaced, I saw three different doctors who concluded it was just my lymphatic system doing its job. Yet my parents pushed for a special diagnostic test called a gallium scan. They wanted to be sure it wasn't a new cancer discovery. I now believe they were prompted by God's Spirit, since it was cancer invading me once again."

The thought of starting over with treatment was overwhelming. Alese was distraught, yet she had to face the cancer head-on. Determination returned—and she needed every ounce of it to face the chemotherapy and stem cell transplant that awaited her.

The "conditioning chemotherapy" given to make her cancer free before the stem cell transplant was performed gave a new definition to the word *sick*. The day after her first treatment, her hair, eyebrows, and eyelashes fell out. It was five days of hospital horror. She was then allowed to go home before the stem cell transplant was to occur. But after only three days with her family, she developed a fever that landed her back at the hospital for another twenty-three days. "This too shall pass," were the words Alese used to encourage herself, and she trusted in the Lord.

"People who are confronted with life-threatening diseases view life much differently than prior to their illnesses. All the priorities change; what was once important seems irrelevant. We must not waste our lives. I now realize how brief our time on earth really is, and what we do while we're here really matters."

So do relationships. "My sister Shallyn and I used to fight and argue, but when I got sick, that all stopped. The stuff that seemed so important before now was so trivial, and we both realized how much we meant to each other. I don't know what I would have done without her. She gave me a sense of normalcy as we talked about students at school or painted our nails. She always told me how beautiful I looked, even though I was bald and overweight from the steroids."

Time for the stem cell transplant.

Alese spent twenty-nine days in isolation at UCLA Medical Center. With the transplant completed, it was a waiting game to see if her white blood cells would increase, giving her health back to her. Her large hospital room allowed for her parents to be with her the entire time she was in isolation. That helped with the loneliness. "They cared for me when I couldn't care for myself. My mom was very nurturing when I would get violently ill, and my dad always found a way to make me laugh. So many teens rag on their parents unjustly. But if they were in my situation, they would see how loved they truly are. My parents were my anchor throughout the most difficult time of my life, and I'm blessed by their commitment, encouragement, and unconditional love."

Wouldn't it get boring to be in the hospital that long? Yep, so Alese learned to crochet, creating a

## In Her Own Words . . .

Through this whole cancer ordeal, there are several things I have learned that are blessings in my life. Here they are!

Attitude is queen.

Being bald is not as bad as I thought it would be.

A good team of doctors is necessary, but without God you are missing the greatest Physician of all.

Having a family who loves you through thick and thin is incredible.

When you're faced with adversity, you find out who your true friends are.

Follow God's dreams for you and pursue them with unwavering passion—no matter your age or adversity.

Without question, God is good, even when bad things happen.

Knowing people were praying for me and seeing God work on my behalf because of their prayers is beyond words.

I truly believe in miracles.

~ Alese Coco

special blanket, and took up journaling. She never felt envious of those who weren't sick, because she would never wish cancer on anyone.

After Alese was finally released from the hospital, she endured eighteen days of radiation, which left her nauseous the entire time. At the end of all the treatments, physically weak and forty-five pounds lighter, Alese was declared cancer free. Her doctors assured her she would feel totally normal within six months. "Although this journey has been long, it has only illuminated the flame that God has put in my heart."

The score was now Alese 2, cancer 0.

Alese returned to college, and as a big surprise, her parents bought her a metallic charcoal BMW convertible with black leather interior. She was stylin'! And happy! And healthy!

Then the unthinkable.

Five new spots of cancer were detected on her lungs, as well as one on her stomach that was attached to the main artery, making surgery to that area impossible.

Strike three.

Treatment options were running out. Alese's doctors told her they were sorry but there was nothing else they could do for her. That's when they looked into clinical trials. Alese agreed to submit herself to treatment with an experimental drug called SAHA through a clinical trial being conducted at Sloan Kettering Cancer Center in New York. Alese and her family knew she didn't have much time. Alese was watching her good friend Kim die from the same type of cancer. She'd met Kim at UCLA Medical Center, where they'd both received stem cell transplants. Kim was two years younger than Alese, and her Hodgkin's returned for the third time just a few months before Alese was struck the third time. Alese watched her friend get worse and was with her the day she died. She knew the writing was on the wall; her prognosis was the same as Kim's.

Plans for New York were made. They learned of a vacant apartment near the hospital and committed to signing a lease. Flight arrangements were confirmed and doctor appointments scheduled. The Alese Coco Foundation was formed to help pay for treatments and living expenses. Everything appeared to be in place.

Then the call came in. Due to scheduling, they would need to wait eleven days for the surgical removal of the five spots. Then they would leave for New York. Alese and her parents decided to take full advantage of the unwelcome wait. The extra time proved to be on their side. They asked their doctor for one more scan prior to surgery. In the meantime, they issued an all-points prayer alert!

The email I received from Alese's mom read, "We feel this waiting period could be a blessing in disguise, so we have decided to take advantage of this opportunity. With surgery a week and a half away, we requested a follow-up scan. Thankfully, her doctors agreed. So we are asking you to join us and pray this scan will come back clean and Alese's body will be found cancer free. However, if this does not happen, we will not be discouraged, because we know God has a plan that we cannot see. Over the two years of dealing with this disease, we have felt the power of prayer. We know our God is wonderful and faithful to his Word."

Alese welcomed the prayer. Her youth group from church prayed as a group and sent her cards. They even made her a video talking about how they missed her, how they were going to come bust her out of the hospital, and how the girls had lost their fashion sense without Alese around! She also received gifts. Her favorites were all the pajamas she was given, since she literally lived in them! Changing into new, fresh PJ's was fun and a great reminder that she was clothed in love.

But her spirits weren't so bright on surgery day.

All prepped and ready to be wheeled into the operating room, Alese kissed her family. While the doctors were operating, they were astonished. They couldn't find the cancer that had shown up on the scan. So after surgery the scan was repeated.

October 28, 2003, Alese received a call from her doctor. The results of her gallium scan were in. Negative! All spots were gone! She was cancer free! Can you imagine the celebration? Prayer prevailed. Heaven moved!

The final score? Alese 3, cancer 0!

Hey, cancer, three strikes and you're out!

Today, Alese is finishing her college degree in nursing and living each day to the fullest, praising her God every step of the way. "For everything comes from God alone. Everything lives by his power, and everything is for his glory" (Romans 11:36 TLB).

# Hugs from Heaven

Smiling, I cast my eyes upward and said, "Thanks for the hug, Lord." A sunny day, a cool breeze, acing an exam, getting an email from an old friend, having a great parking space open up, finding a lost CD, snagging the last bag of Skittles or Red Hots off the shelf, watching your home team score the winning point, seeing two friends resolve their cat fight and greet each other with smiles. Special things. Unexpected yet welcomed things. I call these hugs from heaven! I can just envision God leaning over on his throne, watching as the "little somethings" he sends down reach you and me.

If you pay attention, you'll see them. You'll notice them. These aren't official blessings as we've defined them or as the Bible defines them, but nevertheless, they feel like blessings! Sometimes it's the seemingly small things that can bring the biggest thrills. Things that make you go, "Yeah, God!" Things that show God's favor. Things that make you reach up and high-five the Lord! I really do this, and I really don't care if someone sees me! See, when you're in relationship with Jesus and are aware that he's with you all the time, you talk to him throughout the day. He's your companion. You share stuff with him. You "celebrate the moments of your life" with him. You high-five him knowing he just sent you a little something. A hug! Resist the temptation to just chalk these things up to coincidence. This will steal the joy of the hug. When you're in Christ's care, there are no coincidences. But there are lots of hugs that will bless your socks off!

# The Blessings Book

One great way to focus on your blessings is to keep a blessings book. Get a blank journal and get ready to fill it with some incredible stuff. If the idea of a whole book sounds overwhelming, start by creating a blessings list. This will give you a jump start! Get alone with God so you can clearly think of all your blessings. Include all the things talked about in this chapter, like Jesus, salvation, forgiveness, eternal life, the fruit of the Spirit, your spiritual gifts, and so on. Next, add the hugs from heaven. Write down every little squeeze! Get the list copied so you can tape it to your bathroom mirror and read it while you blow-dry your hair. Tape a copy inside your locker; it's a great pick-me-up in the middle of your day.

Now take your list and put it in the front of your blessings book. Then every time you receive a new blessing, record it! If you do this regularly, your book will be full before you know it!

Here's an important tip. To get the most out of this experience, you must review your blessings book often. It will help you see how God is working in your life. It will remind you that you're loved and valued by the God of the Universe. It will make you even more aware of his presence and interest in your everyday life. How amazing is that? And it will make your heart happy!

## The B.A.B.E. Checklist

Girlfriend, the most important part of "B Is for Blessed!" is our talk about the meaning of *blessed*. If you have any inkling of doubt in your mind about the fact that you're blessed, then you need to stop right now and go back to the opening pages of this section. Read them again and soak them up! God has done so much for you, and when you see and acknowledge it, life does a turnaround.

This checklist will help bring it all back to you.

> **Need a great pick-me-up in the middle of a long school day? Count your blessings one by one!**

| Yes | No | Almost | |
|---|---|---|---|
| ____ | ____ | ____ | I can describe to another person what it means to be blessed so he/she will understand it from God's viewpoint. |
| ____ | ____ | ____ | I know the difference between natural abilities and spiritual gifts. |
| ____ | ____ | ____ | I've been able to figure out which spiritual gifts I've been given. |
| ____ | ____ | ____ | I've determined an activity or ministry that my spiritual gift is ideal for. |
| ____ | ____ | ____ | I understand that my gifts can change or increase as I mature in my walk with Christ. |
| ____ | ____ | ____ | I'm ready to start a blessings list or book. |
| ____ | ____ | ____ | I see the Holy Spirit alive and at work in me. Exciting! |
| ____ | ____ | ____ | I understand that God has blessed me in many ways. |
| ____ | ____ | ____ | I understand that being blessed doesn't mean having everything I want. |
| ____ | ____ | ____ | I recognize that true blessings are spiritual blessings from God. |
| ____ | ____ | ____ | God's kind of blessings aren't about having lots of stuff. |
| ____ | ____ | ____ | Since I've invited Jesus into my life, I know the Holy Spirit is in me. |
| ____ | ____ | ____ | I appreciate that I can get my sins forgiven immediately when I confess them to the Lord (1 John 1:9). |
| ____ | ____ | ____ | I'm thanking God daily for providing eternal life for me. |
| ____ | ____ | ____ | I welcome the Holy Spirit's work in my life as he does his job of guiding, teaching, and comforting. |
| ____ | ____ | ____ | I'm willing to work with the Holy Spirit in developing the nine fruit he's brought into my life. |
| ____ | ____ | ____ | I have Spirit power in me. |
| ____ | ____ | ____ | I'm recognizing other people's gifts and learning to appreciate them. |

I have a sense that you get this stuff! And just to challenge you a bit, might I suggest that you become an "expert" in your spiritual gift by using it? Develop it! Yep, practice makes perfect! And as you put your gift into action, sprinkle your loving deeds with God's fruit that lives in you! Everyone will be drawn to your babe-a-licious self, which means they'll come that much nearer to Jesus! You go, girlfriend!

4

**e is for**

# eter

# nALLy
## SIGNIFICANT!

# NO EXPIRATION DATE

Have you ever taken a big swig of milk or stuffed a huge spoonful of raspberry yogurt through your lips only to end up with a mouthful of nasty? Gross, huh? It usually happens to me with cottage cheese. My favorite lunch has a tendency to turn bad quickly. But as long as it's still white, I forget the taste can change dramatically. Yuck! In fact, it can be so yuck that I have to go brush my teeth and use mouthwash!

It's wise to keep an eye on expiration dates.

Whether it's food (mostly the refrigerated kind), baking powder (I can't tell you how many times my chocolate chip cookies have turned out flat), sunscreen (it's not very effective past its prime), or valuable coupons (don't you just cringe when you proudly hand the salesclerk your "buy one burger, get one free" coupon only to find out it's not any good anymore?), it's always essential to pay attention to this kind of detail! Lots of things expire. They reach a point when they aren't good anymore. They're temporary. Here today, gone tomorrow.

After all, nothing lasts forever, right?

**Wrong!**

God stuff is eternal. In fact, God is eternal. He's everlasting, infinite, unending, and timeless. He keeps going on and on forever. He isn't bound by time or space or elements. He's constant and ceaseless.

God has created you and me to be eternal too. We were made in his image, remember? Though our bodies will pass away, our spirits and souls will live forever. We will go from earth into eternity. And because we are "in Christ," eternity for us is all about heaven. You and I will never cease to exist, and the entire time we're here on earth, God's got plans for us—plans that matter, plans that make a difference, plans that affect eternity!

**The E in B.A.B.E. is for eternally significant!**

How cool is that?

We don't have an expiration date. No one can flip us over and find an imprint that reads, "Best if used by 9/9/2009." Aren't you glad?

Now, think this through with me. Since we've been created for forever and ever, what would be the best use of our time? How can we invest our energy and emotions in a way that matters? Should we go after things that are temporary, things that are the very opposite of eternal? Or should we invest in things that are eternal—just like us?

Temporary pursuits would be things like having your nails done; being the first in line to see the latest flick; collecting dolls or CDs; working out; satisfying your shopaholic cravings whenever possible; working to be number one; striving to acquire medals, trophies, or crowns; saving your bucks to buy the hottest thing on four wheels. That kind of stuff.

Are these things wrong?

If temporary things occupy most of your thoughts or top your "life's greatest goals" list, then yeah, they are. But if you keep them in balance, it's okay. Pretty nails can make you feel feminine, seeing movies is fun (especially while you munch on popcorn), collections can be wonderful reminders of special times in your life, working out is good for healthy hearts and toned muscles, and wanting to do your best is great. Just remember, temporary things shouldn't take first place in your heart. That place needs to be reserved for things that are eternal.

Here's what Jesus has to say on the topic:

> Do not store up for yourselves treasures on earth, where moth and rust destroy, and where thieves break in and steal. But store up for yourselves treasures in heaven, where moth and rust do not destroy, and where thieves do not break in and steal. For where your treasure is, there your heart will be also.
>
> Matthew 6:19–21 NIV

Jesus makes it clear that earthly or temporary treasures won't last. They will tarnish, break down, go out of style, or lose their value. Plus, you can't take it with you! But heavenly treasures are things no one can mess up or swipe! They're never obsolete or out of style.

This makes me think of Paul, the guy who came face-to-face with Jesus on the road into the town of Damascus. Before he met Jesus, he was all about temporary. Read Acts 9:1–2; Acts 22:1–5; and Philippians 3:4–7. What were Paul's earthly credentials? What was he doing to Christians (people of the Way, as in "Jesus is the Way, the Truth, and the Life")?

Now keep reading in Philippians 3:8–14. How did Paul view his credentials after encountering Jesus (verse 8)?

What became his eternal goals (verses 9–11)?

Paul ends up saying that he now forgets what lies behind (the temporary) and reaches forward to what lies ahead (the eternal). Check out 2 Corinthians 4:18 to read it for yourself.

Temporary pursuits won't last. Temporary stuff won't last. Eternal pursuits will.

So what pops into your mind when you think of eternal pursuits?

How about showing kindness? What about being loving? Maybe praying for someone or helping a friend become a Christian.

Some eternal things can't be seen with your eyes. You may not be able to put them in your scrapbook or list them on your college application. For example, we can't see a person's spirit become new, but we can see her changed lifestyle. We can't see love, but we can see the results of love! We can't see someone's faith, but we can see his determined sense of hope that is fueled by his faith.

Yet some stuff can be seen. You know, things like doing yard work for your elderly neighbor, sharing a Bible story with a classmate, or slipping a witnessing tract in your teammate's locker. Those are eternal activities. So is starting a breakfast prayer group before Sunday school or being part of a mime troop that performs biblical themes or taking all your too-big or too-small clothes to the homeless shelter. These actions produce things that last, things that won't get moth infested or come up missing.

You are eternal. You can choose to do things that count for eternity, things that don't expire, things that matter to God, things that are valuable in God's kingdom, things that glorify God, things that are **significant**.

**Your heart will reflect the things you treasure most. So what do you treasure?**

# NOTHING TO IT?

Nearly seven hundred teen girls landed in the city of Quito, Ecuador, during the summer of 2003. They were eager to see what God had in store for them. Each morning after team devotions, they loaded the buses and headed out to their ministry area of the day. About a week into the trip, one team got a special treat. No, they didn't stop for ice cream or a soda. They were allowed to go into a very poor area high in the hill country that was considered dangerous for Americans. But one of their team interpreters knew the area and many of the people quite well because her mother lived in this village. It was a village that hadn't heard the gospel message, a village that didn't know the kindness of strangers, a village where poverty was high and hope was low. When the team arrived, it was past their lunchtime. They decided to make their peanut butter and jelly sandwiches (the official missionary lunch) before they performed their drama. But as they made their PB and Js, they looked into the faces of the little ones and the elderly who had crowded around them. There was a look of hunger in their eyes. The girls instantly knew they couldn't eat in front of these people, but if they shared their sandwiches, only a few would be fed. They feared a riot. But choosing to forgo their portion of the lunch, they prayed and asked God to make it possible for all to be fed. With a few loaves of bread and several jars of peanut butter and jelly, they got busy making and distributing pieces of sandwiches to the villagers.

To their astonishment, everyone got fed! They had witnessed a God thing. A miracle! They willingly gave up their lunch to feed the hungry, the poor, the needy.

Was it a big deal to pass up the PB and Js? Not really. It was just a measly kind of meal anyway. To the girls, it was something seemingly insignificant. Something quite simple. Yet to the people with empty stomachs, it was quite significant! It was a kindness they wouldn't soon forget. Neither would God.

As each girl offered her food, God was looking down wearing a delighted grin and whispering an attagirl!

# You Matter!

Something that is significant has value. It's important, meaningful, and noteworthy. Just like you!

You are significant in the eyes of God. You are valuable and important. You matter to God. And when you do things he asks you to do, when you obey his commandments, you take on a new kind of significance. The eternal kind! You become eternally significant. You do and say things that point to Jesus and glorify your heavenly Father.

Read Matthew 10:42 and 25:31–46. What kinds of actions were significant to Jesus?

What are the results of these actions? Check out Matthew 5:14–16.

Seemingly simple things become significant when they're done **in Jesus's name** (on his behalf). Anything you do

## In Their Own Words . . .

**If you could do anything for God, what would it be?**

I would love for God to use me in the unreached places of the world. Over three billion people have still not heard the gospel. I would like to be their messenger.

~ Kara

One of my passions is to design and direct a camp for teen girls and teach them how to become godly women. I would be honored if God would use me for that.

~ Andrea

I would like to be a graphic designer for a Christian band or publisher.

~ Kelly

Sports are my passion. God has given me much athletic skill, and I want to use it to point others to him—on and off the field.

~ Lynn

for God, anything you do in the name of Jesus, anything that brings God glory, has eternal significance.

Jesus said that if we . . .

feed the hungry (whether it's a friend who forgot lunch money or the guy on the corner with a "will work for food" sign),

clothe the poor (how about yanking out of your closet all those threads you never wear and donating them to a charity?),

take in the homeless (ever known a teen that got kicked out of her house or maybe just locked out?),

visit the sick (the hospital is full of them, but why not drop in on members of your church or youth group who are under the weather?), or even

offer a cup of cold water (helping others with their basic life needs) **in his name**, it has eternal significance!

Jesus said that what we do for others we do for him! When we serve in his name, it counts for the kingdom of God. And then comes the glory! Our obedience brings glory to God. Isn't that incredible? Do you look at yourself and think, *I can't do anything big for God.* Do you think that only in your wildest imagination could God use you? Do you wish he would give you a sign? Do you dream of the day God does something significant through you? Well, B.A.B.E., your dream is about to become reality!

> No eye has seen,
>   no ear has heard,
> no mind has conceived
>   what God has prepared for those who love him.
>
> 1 Corinthians 2:9 NIV

**Take what God has given you, ask him to bless it, then step out in faith in Jesus's name! You'll love the results!**

# Star Light, Star Bright

You know how it goes. Say it with me. "Star light, star bright, first star I see tonight. I wish I may, I wish I might, get the wish I wish tonight!"

If you've been squeezing your eyes closed and wishing for God to use you, the wishing is over. You're soon to discover God's plan and purpose. If you haven't already, you're going to do something eternally significant *for* God, thus making you eternally significant *to* God! It happened to Jeremiah, and it can happen to you!

Jeremiah wasn't much older than you when God showed up one night and made a mind-boggling statement. "Before I formed you in the womb I knew you, before you were born I set you apart; I appointed you as a prophet to the nations" (Jeremiah 1:5 NIV).

God formed and created Jeremiah (**he was God's idea, and so were you**). God had a reason for bringing Jeremiah into the world, a specific assignment (a real live prophet to speak to the people on God's behalf).

Like with Jeremiah, God planned for you, and he had a pretty specific job in mind for you when he did so. And just like with Jeremiah, God will reveal your job to you. You don't have to wish any longer that God will use you or work through you to accomplish something significant. It's already in the plan! And it's a good plan.

Just like Jeremiah prophesied (he **did** become what God had planned) to the people of Israel, I believe God says the same thing to you and me today:

"For I know the plans I have for you," declares the Lord, "plans to prosper you and not to harm you, plans to give you hope and a future. Then you will call upon me and come and pray to me, and I will listen to you. You will seek me and find me when you seek me with all your heart."

Jeremiah 29:11–13 NIV

To get the full impact of this verse, choose four key words and define them. This is open book, so go grab your dictionary and thesaurus.

**Word**                    **Definition**
1. _____    _____
2. _____    _____
3. _____    _____
4. _____    _____

Now read the verse again and identify God's part and your part.

**God:**

**You:**

See, it's a partnership. God has a plan, and you have to diligently seek him to know that plan. You and God each have a role to play in fulfilling your life assignment.

Knowing this will help you discover that plan and to know that God has eternally significant stuff set aside with your name on it!

No fear, excuse, or rotten past can outdo God's ability to use you when, where, and how he wants!

## Inside Edition:
# CAMPUS ALERT!
# THE BIBLE COMES TO SCHOOL

Do you have a passion to do something eternally significant for Christ?

You, girlfriend, can have an impact for Christ at a place where you plant your feet five days a week!

Yep, your very own school campus can be a great gathering place for the gospel! You might also start up something new or join a group already in motion. Here are some ideas along with informational resources:

**Rally!** Organize the annual September See You at the Pole. This is a time when students gather before school at the flagpole to pray for their schools, friends, communities, and countries. Get informed at www.syatp.com.

**Specialize!** Start a Fellowship of Christian Athletes "huddle." Offering fellowship, discipleship, and evangelism to athletes and coaches, this student-led campus gathering includes Bible study, volunteer work (such as Special Olympics), community outreach, and more. Find out the facts of an official huddle at www.fca.org. (Bonus: FCA summer camps!)

**Join!** Sponsored by Youth for Christ, Campus Life (high school) and Campus Life/MS (middle school) host activities that give students a terrific opportunity to hang out with kids from your school or others.

**Focus!** Conduct an informal survey asking what troubles students about their school or home lives. Then gear your Bible studies to the topics that speak to your peers the most. Check out the FreshResource series published by NavPress, www.navpress.com.

**Encourage!** The life experiences of other teens can be just the right measure of inspiration. Read uplifting articles about teens from www.briomag.com, www.youthspecialties.com, and www .everyschool.com. Then share the stories with your friends.

**Pray!** This may be the most important step before you jump-start the club! Ask a relative, youth leader, or friend to pray consistently and specifically for your mission and for like-minded girls to team up with you to make it happen!

**Action!** Since you know the Holy Spirit has spread his spiritual gifts all around, your club of faithful B.A.B.E.s has the potential to be a real hot spot for his kingdom purposes! Quietly observe other students in action to spot their spiritual gifts, and then discern through prayer how those gifts might best be used.

BTW, here are some gifts that are definitely in play at a campus impact ministry:

**Leadership:** "Motivational B.A.B.E.s" effectively leading others to share and write the campus club mission statement.

**Administration/Helps/Serving:** "Go-to B.A.B.E.s" for organizing gatherings, coordinating outreach efforts, and completing behind-the-scenes work.

**Faith:** "Cheerleading B.A.B.E.s" confidently sharing life experiences that point others up to God and bring him the glory.

**Evangelism:** "E-B.A.B.E.s" living out their passion to rock the school for Christ by leading others to Jesus.

**Hospitality:** "Bubbly B.A.B.E.s" positively overflowing with personality, welcoming spirits, and helping hands.

**Mercy/Exhortation/Encouragement:** "Tenderhearted B.A.B.E.s" attuned to the facial expressions, words, and body language of others, ready to offer a listening ear and God's words of encouragement.

**Wisdom:** "Get-real B.A.B.E.s" who positively and authoritatively apply biblical wisdom to everyday situations.

**Pastor/Shepherd:** "Discipling B.A.B.E.s" guiding and counseling new or fallen Christians into a deeper and right walk with God.

**Intercession:** "Go-between B.A.B.E.s" sensitively lifting up expressed personal needs of students and committing to pray outside the club for particular needs or special events of the club.

**Teaching:** "Message B.A.B.E.s" accepting the assignment of Bible study leader, digging into Scripture, and sharing it.

# Significantly Successful

So exactly **who** determines what's significant and what isn't? Our society teaches us that significance comes with position, power, prestige, and possessions. If you've got the goods, you automatically have clout, status, and importance. Really?

Our culture says that significance is always accompanied by splashy success. **But whose definition of success?** Does public recognition make you successful? Does being on TV do it? Does being wealthy cinch it? If so, then by definition, Paris Hilton, the heiress to the Hilton Hotel fortune, is a huge success. After all, she starred in MTV's *Rich Girls* and Fox's *The Simple Life*, she's worth millions, and her family name gives her prestige and power. Is she a success? Is a girl who plays a dumb blonde and makes a private porn video that ends up on the Internet a success?

Then there's Jessica Simpson. Wealthy? Yes. Talented? Yes. Great hair? Yes. On TV? Yep. But let's be real. In one episode of her show *Newlyweds: Nick and Jessica*, Jessica didn't even understand that the Chicken of the Sea tuna she was eating was tuna! "Is this chicken, what I have, or is this fish?" Apparently, rich chicks don't eat canned tuna. But real people do! I love it—especially the albacore. (Plus, the omega-3 fatty acids in fish are fabulous for your body!)

And let's not overlook the Olsen twins, Mary-Kate and Ashley. I recently read that at the age of eighteen, their clothing, makeup, stationery, and backpack lines were projected to bring in a whopping $1.2 billion in sales. And that doesn't include the big bucks from their movie careers. They're deemed an overwhelming success, yet Mary-Kate wasn't immune to the problem of an eating disorder.

Jessica, Paris, Mary-Kate, Ashley, and many others like them are considered successful by worldly standards. Our culture makes them think they're priceless and precious. What a waste. They're very deceived divas. Paris's string bikini and barely there attire, some of Jessica's trashy and ungodly song lyrics—are these true marks of success in God's opinion?

In God's eyes our significance begins the moment we become his children. Then as we grow in our faith and knowledge of him, he leads us to do things that are significant, meaning things that count for eternity. That leads to the true meaning of success: **to discover God's purpose for you and to do it**! That's real and lasting success—not by the world's standards, but by God's.

But why take my word for it when Jesus himself explains it the same way? Take John the Baptist. He was Jesus's older cousin, set apart before birth for a specific purpose: to announce the coming of God's kingdom and call for people to repent. He spent most of his life in the wilderness eating locusts and wild honey. He was far from a fashion stud in his hairy animal skins and leather belt. He was uncompromising in speaking God's standards, which eventually got him beheaded in his early thirties. Yet Jesus says of him, "Truly I say to you, among those born of women there has not arisen anyone greater than John the Baptist" (Matthew 11:11 NASB).

**When you understand God's purpose for you and discover his calling for your life, you're on your way to being successful!**

Not even close to a success by worldly standards. Yet a great man in the eyes of God because he fulfilled the eternally significant plan that had been divinely prepared for him. That's success. It didn't gain him fame and fortune. He didn't have a limo or a bodyguard. He wasn't served. He was a servant.

Being a successful follower of Jesus is all about serving. Jesus said that he came to earth to serve, not to be served. Yes, the rich and famous like Paris and Jessica have assistants, chauffeurs, chefs, personal trainers, and others who serve them. It seems so impressive, and if we're honest, there's probably a tiny part in each of us that wants that! But that's not what it's about in God's book. Check this out:

> The more lowly your service to others, the greater you are. To be the greatest, be a servant. But those who think themselves great shall be disappointed and humbled; and those who humble themselves shall be exalted.
>
> Matthew 23:11–12 TLB

> Your attitude must be like my own, for I, the Messiah, did not come to be served, but to serve, and to give my life as a ransom for many.
>
> Matthew 20:28 TLB

Confession time. As a high school student, I was involved with lots of service projects—an adopt-a-grandparent program, nursing home bingo parties, food drives for homeless shelters, and stuff like that. But I got a bit spoiled when I was modeling in New York. I got a small taste of worldly success, which whetted my appetite for what I thought at the time were the finer things in life. I loved it when my doorman buzzed my apartment to say my limousine had arrived.

I adored showing up at restaurants where we were seated immediately even though lots of other people were standing in line. Preferential treatment. It made me feel important. But I was weighing that importance on the wrong values system.

Months later, as a result of the Holy Spirit working hard on me, I moved back to the Midwest. I remember foolishly saying to the Lord, "Okay, if I can't be great in this world, then make me great in your kingdom. Use me to do something big for you."

The Lord nailed me immediately. The words of Scripture came instantly to my mind, and the Holy Spirit used them to speak to me.

"Andrea, the greatest of all is the servant of all" (see Mark 10:41–46).

*Servant? Like in serve? As in doing stuff for others instead of them doing for me?* God really had his work cut out for him. It was a hard lesson to relearn, but every day I'm grateful that he isn't a God who gives up on us. Ever! Serving brings joy to both Jesus and me. Don't get confused here—we don't serve so we gain the Lord's acceptance and favor. We're already fully accepted. We serve out of gratitude.

You and I are destined for success. Not the worldly kind, but the godly kind. Not standing to be honored, but kneeling to be humbled. Want to do great things for God? Do an attitude and latitude turnaround! Easy? No. Worth it? Absolutely. You'll discover exactly what the **finer** things in life really are!

# More than a Clay Lump

To the average person, it looks like a dirty glob. Its dull surface certainly draws no special attention. Its irregular shape is curious, but one passes it off quickly. It's easily overlooked. It's a lump, a lump of clay.

One person sees the clay through different eyes. He envisions something far beyond the imagination. He envisions you. And me. One of his kids.

God is the Potter; we are the clay. It's his job to work with us until we finally become moldable in his hands. Once we are moldable, he shapes us into the form that best fits with his plan for us. We're shaped differently from others, shaped according to his purpose for us.

Some of us are plates. Some are cups, and some bowls or even vases. Some are candlesticks, and some are soap dishes. It all depends on the Potter.

Be assured that we're all equally valuable, equally needed, and equally appreciated. There's no partiality with God (Romans 2:11).

To the Potter, you're so much more than a dull clay glob. You're the work of his hands, shaped and ready for use. Yes, use! Everyone gets used by the Potter in some way. However, the **amount** you're used is partially up to you. God is looking for availability, flexibility, and faithfulness. These things are up to you and me to offer to him. Each one of us has an equal opportunity to be used by God. It makes no difference what year we were born or where we live or how much we know. Jesus is looking for our **availability**, **flexibility**, and **faithfulness** so he can give us kingdom assignments.

173

# So, what do those words mean?

**Availability** is simply choosing not to be so scheduled and stressed that when the Holy Spirit whispers an instruction in your ear, you have to brush him off. Availability says, "Here I am, Lord. Send me!"

**Flexibility** is a willingness to go with the Holy Spirit flow. To allow for his agenda and not stress over a change of plans. It's about trying not to get caught in a rut. It's letting go of the control. It's all about surrendering to the Lord.

**Faithfulness** is about coming through, finishing up, and not quitting—even when the going gets tough. Luke 16:10 says that as we're faithful in completing God's small assignments, we're qualified for larger ones. (The smaller assignments help us get our attitudes straight so that when we get the larger assignments, we'll remember that they're about God, not about us.)

"Become blameless and pure, children of God without fault in a crooked and depraved generation, in which you shine like stars in the universe as you hold out the word of life." ~ Philippians 2:14–16 NIV

# I Want To Be a ...

"What do you want to be when you grow up?"

That question starts at an early age. It sends the minds of young ones into a wonderland of possibility. A mermaid. A fairy princess. A ballerina.

As maturity sets in, the responses become more realistic. A nurse. A firefighter. A mom. A professor. An astronaut. A senator. A professional athlete. A missionary.

When you were younger, what did **you** want to be? Why?

Growing up, we girls are great at playing dress up. We put on our mom's shoes and lipstick, adorn our necks with strings of plastic beads, pinch Grandma's clip-ons onto our earlobes, toss on a floppy hat or an old wig, and enter the world of make-believe. Pretending becomes our play. Imaginations run wild, and we can get wrapped up in a role for hours.

Little girls grow up, but they still get asked those same questions.

"So you're going to graduate next year?" "Where are you going to college?" "What's your major?" "What do you want to become?"

Heaven forbid that we say, "I don't know yet." That answer can have a way of making us feel like we don't know what we're doing, that there's confusion in our pretty little heads, or that we're directionless and therefore headed toward the waterfall of failure. Many girls pop out a reply just to hush the person with the inquiring mind: "A veterinarian." "A legal assistant." "A dental hygienist."

All those questions can send you into a tailspin, causing you to question yourself!

"Hey, what *am* I going to be? What *do* I want to do?"

Herein lies the problem.

**We're asking the wrong questions!**

See, we're conditioned at a young age to think in terms of "I," to be self-centered or self-focused. What do *I* want, what are *my* hopes and dreams, where do *I* want to be in ten years, what do *I* want to accomplish. I . . . I . . . I . . . I . . . I! Me . . . me . . . me . . . me!

We're trained to ask the wrong questions!

What happens when we ask the wrong questions? We get the wrong answers!

What happens when we ask the wrong questions of the wrong person (someone other than God)? Double whammy! That's a surefire setup for life to potentially explode in our faces! It can lead us down the wrong path and get us completely off track! It can cause us to be less than our best! Not good!

### All about Me

Asking myself all those "I" questions led me to believe it was all about me! It could be happening to you too.

When I was a freshman, I was selected to do freeze modeling (formerly called mannequin modeling) for a small store at our local mall. As a junior, I landed a coveted spot on the teen board of a huge department store. I gained lots of training that fed my one desire in life: to be a "real" model (one who is signed to a reputable agency and actually gets paid—and pampered too).

After I graduated, my parents required me to go to college for a year before I pursued modeling, so I did. But then I attended a modeling school and began to prep for a big convention in New York City. Yes, I was ecstatic that I was offered a contract with Wilhelmina Models, Inc. It was everything I wanted. Oh, yes, I had talked it over with God. I told him exactly what I wanted him to do for me. I filled him in on my plans and expected him to bless them. I had created my own agenda without consulting the Lord first.

To make a long story short, let's just say I was living my dream but something wasn't right. Deep down I had little sense of fulfillment. No contentment. It didn't seem to matter that I'd graced the cover of *Hairdo* magazine or *Diet & Exercise* magazine. I didn't feel I'd accomplished my life's destiny just because I'd

**In my misery, I cried to the Lord, and he showed me that I was on the wrong road! Mine! He clearly laid it out in front of me: I could keep doing my own thing and be miserable, or I could seek his plan for my life. The choice was mine. The choice is yours.**

been in a national TV commercial and strutted down a few designers' runways. Instead, I sensed a vacant spot in my soul that was in need of being filled.

Eventually that empty spot was filled when I shifted my focus and started asking the right set of questions and asking them of the right person.

You guessed it. That right person is God!

### All about Him

Here are the right questions to ask of the right person:

God, what do **you** want me to do with my life?

What do **you** have in mind for me?

How do **you** want to use the natural talents, special abilities, and spiritual gifts you've given to me?

Heavenly Father, what can I do for **you**?

How do **you** want me to impact **your** kingdom while I'm here on earth?

You see, the one who created you, designed you, put his stamp of approval on you, and blessed you with natural talents, special abilities, and spiritual gifts did so for a reason! God created you *on* purpose and *for* a purpose!

Back in section one ("B Is for Beautiful!"), we established the fact that you're a divine diva, handcrafted by the Master Designer. You're his work

## In His Own Words . . .

The easiest way to discover the purpose of an invention is to ask the creator of it. The same is true for discovering your life's purpose: Ask God. Nothing matters more than knowing God's purposes for your life, and nothing can compensate for not knowing them.*

~ Rick Warren

*Now that you've graduated from *this* book, you're ready to take on *The Purpose Driven Life* by Rick Warren. (Check out this quote on pages 20, 30 of *The Purpose Driven Life*.)

of art. He gave you intricate details that make you one of a kind. He chose your look, your height, your hair color, your hip size! He personally planned the date of your grand entrance into this world. No doubt about it—you were created on purpose.

God personally planned for you. He does everything on purpose. (Of course, Satan tries to weasel his wicked way in and mess up God's plans, but what he does isn't permanent. Ultimately, God's plan prevails.) God does everything for a reason.

He's not like you and me. He doesn't look back and say, "What did I do that for?" or "Where was my brain on that one?" One word you won't hear slip through God's lips is "Oops." He doesn't goof up. He's organized. He's a planner. He's intentional. He's purposeful. He planned for you, and he has a plan for you!

Your life is intentional. You're here for a purpose. I want you to say, "I'm here for a purpose" out loud. Not just once, three times! Go ahead.

Knowing this fact deep within your heart is your jumping-off point into a life that's so worth it, a life that sets you up to be the best version of yourself possible—the God version of you.

Yet you end up struggling to find that purpose if you ask the wrong questions, if you ask the wrong person, and if you search for answers in the wrong places. That's exactly where lots of people get tripped up. Will you let it happen to you? I hope not! Seek God's agenda for you. After all, the one who created you knows what he created you to do!

> You saw me before I was born and scheduled each day of my life before I began to breathe. Every day was recorded in your Book!
>
> Psalm 139:16 TLB

So you see, it all starts with God. It all stays with God. It all ends with God. It's all about God. It's not about you.

**Live your life on earth the same way Jesus lived his—intentionally!**

# LIFE SCRIPTS

Have you ever auditioned for something? It can be freaky. Your heart is pulsating at the speed of light, your throat is dry as the Sahara, your palms are dripping wet, and your stomach decides to do the butterfly dance. And all of this occurs before you even walk into the audition room.

Once you're there in front of the director, you hope to do your best, but undoubtedly something horrid happens. You trip, you say your name wrong, you laugh and a little thing flies out your nose. Nice.

Trying out for something can make us a bit insecure: *Will I be good enough? Will I be better than the competition? Have I prepared correctly? Will the director like me?*

Relax! When it comes to God, no auditions are necessary. No tryouts! No insecurity meltdowns!

You've already made the cut, you're in, and you have a part waiting for you! In fact, every single believer has a role in God's production. He has written your life script and chosen you for the lead part!

This is where walking with God gets exciting. Every day is an adventure unlike any other kind of adventure. Once you get serious about Jesus really being the leader of your life and you consciously choose to listen and watch for him, your life will take on deeper meaning and greater purpose.

So the first thing I want you to be aware of is this: God has two roles for you in his script. He has a general role for you as part of the cast (body of Christ, the family of God), and he has a specific role—a personal lead part—for you to play. Let's dive into the general cast stuff first.

God has carefully spelled out your general role in the script. What script? The Bible! It contains all the basics concerning your part, your placement, your purpose. Read it carefully and you'll see exactly where you enter the stage and what you are to do. Don't fret about knowing the perfect way to play the part; just look around you. There will be others in the family of God fulfilling the same role you are. It's cool. We're all in this together. Every believer is in the cast.

### The General Cast

Let's open the script so you can get a feel for what your character will be doing, what role you'll play as a general cast member in God's production. These are things he has scripted for all of his cast members—all of his children. We'll start together, and then you can discover a ton more as you read the Bible. Hopefully, you're already aware of—and even doing—lots of these things! You might want to get a special notebook to keep track of your discoveries and then put them in a computer file so they'll be at your fingertips. Whenever you see an instruction given to all believers, jot it down. It's part of God's plan and purpose for your life. Here are a few examples.

**Help those in need!** Sure, you can sign up for volunteer work at the local Gleaners, sling a hammer with Habitat for Humanity, or join your youth group for the next mission trip. But in your everyday life, how about just "being where you are"? That means keeping your eyes, ears, and heart open to new opportunities to put your love for Jesus into action right where you are each day. No deed is too small for the Lord's big kingdom! (See Romans 12:8; Galatians 6:10.)

**Honor your parents!** Honoring means being respectful, and that means being considerate. When your parents set a specific time to be home, before you respond with those well-rehearsed words attempting to justify why you should be allowed to come home later, think how you might instead bless the moment. So instead of staging a protest march, you can smile, offer a gentle hug, and speak words of gratitude,

"Thank you, Dad, for letting me go. I really appreciate you. You can count on me to be home just when you expect me." (See Proverbs 4:1–5; 10:1; 15:1.)

**Stay pure!** Think through what it means to you personally to be pure. Then match up your thoughts with God's by doing a word search on *pure*, *purity*, and *purify* using a concordance and your Bible. When you're ready to commit, write your promise to God. You might wish to tuck this note inside your dresser drawer as a daily reminder. This is a script worth memorizing! (See 2 Timothy 2:21.)

**Be like Jesus!** "For those God foreknew he also predestined to be conformed to the likeness of his Son" (Romans 8:29 NIV). Read through the four Gospels observing Jesus's actions and reactions, and you'll get plenty of ideas on this one.

**Team up with believers!** "Don't become partners with those who reject God" (2 Corinthians 6:14 Message). When it comes to tight-knit situations like a best friend or a prom date, keep fellow cast members closest to you.

**Be honest!** When asked a question, answer truthfully. Think how much value you place on someone else's sincere reply. It doesn't take a high IQ or a fast-thinking-on-your-feet mentality to be honest! There's no script to memorize, because the truth just bubbles up naturally and quickly! "We can say with confidence and a clear conscience that we have been honest and sincere in all our dealings" (2 Corinthians 1:12 NLT; see Proverbs 12:22).

**Pray for others!** The script is clear on this one. We are to lift others up to the Lord, praying for their health, personal needs, spiritual commitment, and more. (See James 5:13–16.)

Have you grasped the basic idea? Is the script starting to make more sense? I hope you're excited to dig into the script with a whole new set of eyes, looking for your entrances and exits, looking for your general role, your purpose. No big deal if you ever lose your place or forget a line or two—just ask the Director! Really! He won't snap or ridicule you. He's not like that. In fact, the script even says, "If any of you lacks wisdom, let him ask of God, who gives to all generously and without reproach, and it will be given to him" (James 1:5 NASB). The Director wants you to do your best, so he's available 24/7 to give you wise insight, guidance, and encouragement.

### The Starring Role

You've dreamed of it, and there it is! A dressing room with your name on it. You don't have a bit part; it's a starring role. You're about to have the time of your life. This will be the performance that will secure your Golden Globe! All of heaven will turn in their vote by private ballot, and your name will be read on the big night! All you need is the right approach—a willingness to do what it takes!

Discovering the lead role, the specific role, your own starring role takes more than just casually reading the script and observing others. You'll need some private coaching sessions—just you and the Director. He'll reveal your specific role, train you, and equip you for the part.

Okay, the script gives you general parts to play as a cast member, but it doesn't necessarily spell out the specific part God wrote just for you. It doesn't speak to each person's special role, his or her star performance. You won't find a verse that reads, "Attend Harvard University to study medicine because I [God] plan to use you to discover the cure for cancer" or "Go to the mission field right out of high school."

This is where your personality, natural talents, special abilities, and spiritual gifts come into play. Let's say you have a natural ability as a dancer and the spiritual gift of evangelism—you want others to know your Jesus! So when you dance your recitals, you do it to a Christian song that speaks of knowing the Lord. Or maybe you get a kick out of little kids, and you have the gift of teaching. The Director may have you lead a Sunday school class, help at children's church, or develop a backyard Bible club during the summer for your neighborhood kids.

**We are God's ambassadors!
We represent heaven here on earth!**

Sixteen-year-old Carrie is down with soccer. She loves the game, and she's good. Last summer she discovered a ministry that goes into other countries teaching soccer camps for kids. The players demonstrate skills and moves that pertain to soccer, but they demonstrate the love of God and the gospel of Jesus that pertains to eternal life. What a great combo.

Are you catching on?

Let's take it a step farther.

### Playing Your Part

The part written just for you will come straight from God, who will direct you through the Holy Spirit, who lives inside you. In fact, in the script there will be a note stating, "See Director." That's your first step.

### Step One: Consult the Director

Make your way immediately and directly to his personal chambers. He'll be expecting you with great excitement. He knows that when you intentionally look to him first in your life, you're serious about knowing and following the plans reserved for you alone. He loves that! Grab your Bible and read Matthew 6:33. What happens when you put God first?

Here's Proverbs 3:6 from *The Living Bible*:

In everything you do, put God **first**, and he will **direct you** and crown your efforts with success.

Amazing! Put God first in everything! For instance, put him first in your thoughts. Before your feet touch the floor, send up a "Good morning, Father." Put him first in your day. Grab your Bible and a cup of cocoa, and spend some quality time with him. Invite him into every aspect of your day; pray for the activities, class assignments, and relationships you'll encounter in the upcoming twenty-four hours. Put him first in your decision making. Ask for

"God, who began a good work within you, will continue his work until it is finally finished."
~ Philippians 1:6 NLT

his wisdom to receive guidance in every situation (James 1:5). See how putting God in the honored spot of your heart will help you detect his plan? Intentionally staying tight with the Director will help you catch all your cues!

## Step Two: Study the Script with Intensity

You'll find clues to your starring role tucked into the Bible. Observe how your Director-God has used others in their starring roles. It will help you understand what he thinks, how he crafts roles for specific people, and what types of things matter to his heart. The more you know the Director, the easier it will be to detect how he may design your specific role and use you. But that's not all. The more you know God, the easier it will be to trust him when he shows you what he wants you to do. Trust is necessary. It's the core of a tight, sold-out, radical relationship with God.

I firmly believe that God's presence is with the Bible. When you open it up and draw near to him, he will draw near to you (James 4:8). It's a promise, B.A.B.E.! Here are a few quick tips for studying the script:

1. **Read it daily.** Find a place with few distractions so you can focus and sense when the Holy Spirit is speaking to you from the Scriptures. Use a version you like. The New International Version, the New Living Translation, and the New American Standard Bible are good choices. The Message is good for additional reading.

2. **Have a plan.** Read five verses or five chapters. Read one chapter of Proverbs with five chapters of Psalms (you'll finish in thirty-one days and can start over). Or you could follow *Brio* magazine's Bible reading plan, found in the back of the magazine each month. Just don't hit and miss.

3. **Be a student.** Students study. Use a study Bible like the Life Application Study Bible (choose your version). It will have great explanations, maps, and profiles. A Bible commentary and Bible dictionary will enhance your study. If you find it dull or boring, you're not digging deep enough!

4. **Keep a spiritual journal.** Keep track of what you're studying and how it speaks to you. It will be an amazing blessing to look back and see all that God is teaching you.

5. **Join a Bible study.** This makes studying the Bible fun and intriguing. You can learn from what others are learning. My sincere suggestion: join an all-girl group. Coed groups often hinder girls from being open and honest.

### Step Three: Seek Him in Prayer

As you chat with the Director and pore over the script, pray, pray, pray! I'm not talking just a pop-up prayer, but earnest and deeply sincere prayer. James 5:16 says, "The earnest prayer of a righteous man has great power and wonderful results" (TLB). Earnest and sincere, intense and fervent prayer—this is called "seeking." Pray to God with diligence. Seek him with your whole heart (Jeremiah 29:13). That's the kind of seeking needed to discover your starring role. Besides, it's a promise. You do your part, God does his part!

### Step Four: Listen for His Voice

When my girlfriend calls me, she just starts talking without identifying herself. That's because she really doesn't need to. It's a formality she can skip because I talk to her so often. I instantly recognize her voice. That's how it can be between you and God! Remember, you're in a **relationship** with the Father, Jesus, and the Holy Spirit. It's two-way. You talk and he listens. Then he talks and you listen. You *can* get to the place where you hear him. No, it won't be an audible voice (though God could do that if he wanted to), but more like an inner knowing or thoughts that come to your mind that aren't from you. Of course, you need to run all these thoughts through the sieve of the Scriptures, because God will never say anything opposite of what's in the Bible. You must understand that! There are many messages and philosophies floating around out there that sound good but are only half true. Compare them to the Bible so you know the whole truth!

And understand this promise from John 10: Jesus is your Shepherd, and you're one of his sheep. His sheep hear his voice! Open up your Bible and read it for yourself!

**Earnest: serious, passionate, and purposeful**
**Fervent: with great intensity of feeling and enthusiasm**
**Sincere: genuine, honest, heartfelt, and pure in motives**

## Step Five: Watch Where He Is Working

When you truly follow steps 1–4, you'll see evidence of God's leading, and you'll be able to trust it. You'll see situations and circumstances come together in a way that only God could have arranged! It will be a God thing, and you'll know it!

Applying these five steps will get you on the way to discovering the parts that have been written just for you—your starring role! This, my friend, is when living for God, being a follower of Jesus, gets really exciting. That day-to-day interaction where you sense him leading you—even the nudges you get to help your sister with her homework—can get you so jazzed. It makes every day an adventure. It turns ordinary into extraordinary. It takes a typical event and turns it into an eternally significant experience! That's the kind of God you serve, B.A.B.E.!

Is something stirring inside of you? Perhaps as you read through this section you're realizing that you aren't as close to the Lord as you want to be or once were. Perhaps you've let the whole Bible thing slip and prayer is just a dull few minutes of fainthearted "help me" or "bless me" requests. If that's where you are, are you ready for something way more meaningful? Do you want that one-on-one intimate relationship with your heavenly Father, the one Jesus died for, the one the Holy Spirit in you makes possible? If so, are you ready to dedicate or rededicate yourself to the relationship? Are you willing to make the time and effort required to have an alive, adventurous life with the Lord? If so, this prayer is for you:

Holy and loving Father, I want to live my life for you. I want to put you in first place. I want to know you, serve you, and be eternally significant for you. I don't want my life to be all about me, but to be all about you. Please forgive me for being wishy-washy and noncommitted to my time in your Word and time seeking you in prayer. Open my spiritual eyes to see you and my spiritual ears to hear you. Fill me anew with your Holy Spirit that I might become all you have planned for me to be. Please use me according to your will. I thank you now, and I praise you.

In Jesus's name I pray, amen.

Signature: _____

Date: _____

# Endless Options

Okay, B.A.B.E., you now know that your general role as a cast member is found in the Bible. Your specific role is discovered as you stay tight with the Lord. But what kinds of things might God direct you to do?

I'm so glad you asked!

As I already mentioned, this is the fun part—the adventure of living directed by God's Spirit! Keep in mind that God's assignments for you will incorporate the spiritual gifts and special abilities that you discovered in "B Is for Blessed!" (section 3). God has equipped you and will fine-tune your training as you go!

Now let's brainstorm. How might God use you?

~ God might use you to speak a word of kindness to brighten someone's day.

~ He might use you to help with crafts or puppets at Vacation Bible School.

~ A mission trip to another country for the purpose of sharing the Good News of Jesus may be on his agenda.

~ Perhaps you'll be asked to put hands and feet on your faith by building a home, a schoolhouse, a corn bin, bathrooms, a pigpen, a stick fence—you never know what God may have you do!

~ God may show you who needs your gentle words of encouragement, then let you know when and how to share them.

~ Maybe he'll use you to offer to pray for a classmate who's going through a hard time.

~ Perhaps he'll use you to organize a food drive to help feed the homeless, and maybe someday work to oversee relief aid in impoverished or war-torn countries!

~ Maybe he'll use you to write strong moral articles for your school newspaper and someday write books or scripts that teach Christian values.

~ Perhaps he'll use you to lead or start a Bible club on your school campus, a club that will introduce other students to Jesus.

~ Maybe God will send you to the nursing home to paint elderly ladies' fingernails, to love on these ladies, touch them, and sing with them while you paint.

~ You may be God's chosen candidate for starting a study group instead of getting sucked into the temptation to cheat on tests.

~ Growing your hair super long then cutting it and sending it to Locks of Love to be used to make a wig for a child with cancer might be what he asks you to do.

These are just a few ice chips off the tip of the iceberg! The possibilities are endless!

Your turn! List some ways God might use you based on your spiritual gifts, passions, and special (natural) talents:

God's options are endless! He'll never run out of assignments and roles designed just for you! Whether they seem big or small to you, they all matter to God! The important thing is to do them. The important thing is be faithful. Then in the end, when we all stand before God, we'll watch as our deeds are put to the fiery test. Whatever we've done for God—for eternity—those things will pass the test. Then we'll be rewarded for our eternally significant actions.

**Your future is full of possibility and promise!**

# Every Day Is Eternity

Just one more point I want you to get before we move on.

God wants every moment of your life to be eternally significant. He wants this new way of looking at your existence here on earth to permeate and flood each part of your life. This is easy once you train your spiritual eyes to see things from heaven's vantage point!

Begin to ask,

How can I use this situation to store up treasure in heaven?

How can I turn this assignment/required task into an opportunity to share about God's love or his peace or his awesomeness?

How can I be an example of someone who is living for God right here on my swim team (or tennis or basketball or cross-country or whatever)?

How can I make even my small actions and decisions count for Jesus?

When you ask these types of questions and look at life through eternity's eyes, you will live out this very important fact. There isn't supposed to be a separation between your school life and your spiritual life, your social life and your spiritual life, your sports life and your spiritual life, your love life and your spiritual life. You aren't to act like you have two separate lives. It's all one life, one single-minded life that's lived with an undivided heart.

Every day, every moment, every action, every word that comes out of your mouth is about your spiritual life. It's about your relationship with Jesus. It's about your eternal significance. Invite the Holy Spirit to be part of what you're doing; then pay attention to his presence—be mindful that he's actually there with you. (Because he is!) He'll show you how you can make more stuff in your life count for eternity. Take his hand and hold on. It's going to be a great ride!

# PREP TIME

*But wait, I've got a life! How can I balance seeking God and cramming for my science exam?*

I thought you might be thinking that, so let's talk it out. You've noticed that to know God's plan and purpose created specifically for you requires doing things that require time. Quality time. Quantity time. But here's the cool thing. As you're seeing both the general and specific roles God has for you, they will help you direct your time, energy, and effort toward the best activities and actions.

That was a mouthful! Broken down, it basically means this. When you know God's specific role for you, you'll be able to make wise choices about activities, clubs, teams, and other potential involvements. And when life piles up on you, your role serves as a guide, helping you cut back on activities and involvements that distract from spending time with God and fulfilling what God has called you to do. It truly makes life more focused, which makes it less hectic. It wipes out that out-of-control feeling. You won't feel so stressed or so fragmented. That's a good thing!

I watched Danielle make some tough choices her sophomore year. She was a gifted writer and excelled in her journalism class. When she was offered the position of front-page editor of the school newspaper, she was shocked and speechless with excitement. She'd been feeling that God was going to use her gifts for this type of thing. She could have greater influence for him in this position. But it was a big job with much responsibility. She had to reevaluate her schedule and activities. She was up to the task even though she realized it would mean forfeiting the dance class she'd signed up for and possibly cutting down on her babysitting jobs.

Every one of us has the same twenty-four hours each day. Pray about your involvements, and do your best to keep tracking with your areas of talent and spiritual gifts.

I recently read on a *Brio* Girl search application about a girl who gave up being the starting center on the school basketball team her senior year so she could spend more time preparing for the group of sixth-graders she was discipling. Another girl quit tennis to be the president of Fellowship of Christian Athletes. Bold moves. These are tough choices. They're the mark of commitment.

Shannon Kubiak chose not to do the dating thing in junior high or high school so she would steer clear of distractions that might steal her affections. She chose to keep them Christ-centered so she could be a serious student of the Bible and available for the things God was calling her to do. One of those things was to write a book. Before Shannon graduated from college, her first book, *The Divine Dance,* was published. She has written several more since then, and they rock! Take a look at www.shannonkubiak.com.

Shannon did something brave. She jumped in with both feet. God isn't just a part of her life, God *is* her life. Jesus isn't on the fringes. He's not just in the middle. He permeates her whole life. She became a young woman God could use for more assignments because she purposely prepared herself. Read that sentence again!

List the activities, commitments, and relationships that would have to change for Jesus to *be* your life:



Pray and create an action plan. Record it here:

Define the word *uncompromising* and what it means to you:


Training yourself to become all God wants, becoming a young woman he can use for his greater glory, and experiencing true abundant life in Christ takes guts. Being different, going against the crowd, standing for godly principles isn't easy. Refusing to cheat, pass along gossip, get drunk, get dragged down into an unhealthy dating relationship, or wear belly-baring tops is tough. Choosing to be honest, honoring your body as God's temple, staying single, or making curfew may make you an oddity among some of your peers. But you, B.A.B.E., have got what it takes.

You've got a solid self-esteem that's based on who you are in Christ, and you know you have value and his full acceptance. You know God has given you gifts and talents and abilities for a spiritual reason—an eternally significant purpose. That gives you the inner strength and a calm confidence to do some really amazing stuff! The sense of accomplishment, purpose, and inner fulfillment you'll feel far outweighs everything else.

When you're serious about serving Jesus, he isn't just part of your life, he *is* your life!

# AD LIBS

You'll excel in your role if you say yes to the part God chooses for you. See, I know from experience that at first glance the role or part you're assigned might not be what you had in mind! Some roles will require letting go of your agenda, your plan, your way of doing things, and signing on with God's. These are called a sacrifice, a living sacrifice!

> Offer your bodies as living sacrifices, holy and pleasing to God—this is your spiritual act of worship.
>
> Romans 12:1 NIV

It's about doing what the Lord wants you to do, here and now, while you're alive and kickin'! It's about trusting his wisdom so much that you can take your role, embrace it, and perform it wholeheartedly. You'll need to develop patience, waiting for the Director to give the cue so you know when and where your role will be played and played most effectively. Too many people mess up here. They want to rush ahead, get out on the stage and perform what they want, where they want, how they want. They may try to imitate someone else's role or even take over a role they were never meant to have! Don't let it happen to you! Don't ad lib! To ad lib means to make it up as you go without consulting the Director. That would be the wrong move.

It happened to me. When I was younger, I pursued pageants and modeling. I boldly told God what I wanted and begged him to bless it and make it happen. And for a while it did happen. But eventually I was miserable! I made the huge mistake of never asking the Lord what *his* plans were for me. That was ignorant and stupid. God alone knew the plan for my life, and I didn't even bother to ask him. He is our **Maker**; therefore,

**"For God is working in you, giving you the desire to obey him and the power to do what pleases him."** ~ Philippians 2:13 NLT

he knows what we're **made for**! So beware. Getting off on our own can happen so easily as we're enticed by the attitudes of our world.

Of course, if that ever happens, the Director will continually work to get you back into your specific role, the role that will fulfill you, bring you contentment and great joy. He never wants you off the script or even quitting the production altogether! He loves you, seeks after you, forgives you, and even forgets your mess-ups and missed cues.

So what does it take to be able to say yes to what God chooses for you?

Sacrifice! And another *S* word will prove invaluable. It's *submission*. Submission means the willingness to say, "Father, if this will accomplish your purposes, then okay. I really want what you want." Jesus had to say that. He had to submit. He willingly made the ultimate sacrifice, yet going to the cross wasn't easy for him. There in the Garden of Gethsemane, he pleaded with his Father to take the cup, the assignment, the cross, away from him. Submission came. Then those famous words, "Not my will, but yours be done." The results were worth it. I believe you'll discover the same thing. Go with what you believe God is leading you to do. And please, stay out of ad lib alley!

---

# Encore!

Some people will dig the way you're making a conscious effort to serve the Lord and choosing to be eternally significant. But some won't. Doing the right thing, the godly thing, might make you unpopular with your peers. You may not get accolades or attagirls. In fact, you might very well get teased or even put down for being what you truly are—a goody-goody! Please understand that if you're called a G-G, it's a huge compliment from eternity's perspective. Yes, I really did say compliment. Really, it means that others notice you're being like Jesus. Yep. Acts 10:38 says that Jesus went around doing good! Jesus and you, you and Jesus, going around doing good! Let the roar from heaven drown out any protests, and hear the saints cheering, "Encore! Encore!" That's right. Just keep it up, B.A.B.E. After all, doing good is exactly what you're here for!

"For we are God's masterpiece. He has created us anew in Christ Jesus, so that we can do the good things he planned for us long ago." ~ Ephesians 2:10 NLT

"Remember, it is better to suffer for doing good, if that is what God wants, than to suffer for doing wrong!" ~ 1 Peter 3:17 NLT

# Roll the Credits

Sometimes I like staying in the theater after a movie has ended so I can read the credits. That's when you really get to find out who is behind the scenes making it all happen. Kind of like the Oz—you know, the wizard guy.

That's the person who deserves the real credit.

That person in your life, my life, and the life of every believer is God. He gets the credit, and he gets the glory for everything we do. In fact, bringing glory to God is to be one of our goals in life. Look at what Jesus said:

> Let your light shine before men in such a way that they may see your good works, and glorify your Father who is in heaven.
>
> Matthew 5:16 NASB

You can bring glory to God! Does that get you excited? Does it boggle your mind that you, little ol' you, can behave in ways and do things that point others to the One who is your purpose and motivation in this life on earth?

Don't freak. Glorifying God isn't about being perfect. If he thought we were capable of being perfect, he wouldn't have sent Jesus to die for our mess-ups. No, glorifying God isn't about that. So what's it about? Let's check with Jesus again.

Let's eavesdrop on his conversation with his Father.

> I have brought you glory on earth by completing the work you gave me to do.
>
> John 17:4 NIV

What does that mean? It means that Jesus fulfilled all the eternally significant assignments the Father gave him to do. And therefore, God was glorified. That's how it worked with Jesus, and that's how it works with us. When we fulfill our God-given purpose in life, we glorify our Father. Everything counts, whether we're in our general role (doing stuff like loving others, serving them, choosing morality, honoring our parents) or in our specific role (doing the stuff God speaks directly to us). It all counts. It all brings him glory.

God created you, God saved you, God filled you with his Spirit, and God equips and strengthens you to do everything he has planned for you. Who else would deserve the credit? Not you. Not me. God alone.

Romans 11:36 says you were made for God's glory. It's your ultimate purpose. And when you accomplish that purpose, you're going to hear those six words upon your entrance into heaven, six words that will rock your soul:

Well done, good and faithful servant!

Matthew 25:21 NIV

And then, my friend, you'll enter into the Father's joy. When you choose to do what God calls you to do, it glorifies him, but it also gives him great joy. He delights in you and then invites you to share in the joy. *For real?* For real.

## This Is God's Deal:
# THE BaRLOWGIRL STORY

Rebecca Barlow, Bec to her sisters, never imagined that at age twenty-four (or thirty-four for that matter), she'd be playing bass and singing in an all-girl rock band. She was the shy, quiet one. Her struggle with low self-esteem and a high level of self-doubt added up to deep feelings of self-dislike. "I would never go on stage by choice. It wasn't me. I had this fear, and I just thought everyone hated me. Really, I felt worthless and stupid, but this is not how God viewed me."

Alyssa Barlow, or Liz, had dreamed of lights, cameras, and action. She wanted Broadway. Excelling at both dance and acting seemed to confirm her plans. Playing various roles suited her well. Reading from a script—someone else's words—fit her style, or her insecurities. Being real with others and speaking from her heart in front of thousands—without a script—wasn't on her agenda. "I would not have chosen to be in the band, but God enables me to get up there and be vulnerable, sharing my heart with all those people looking at me."

Lauren Barlow, lovingly called Lolo by her older sisters, was just finishing high school when the all-girl rock band idea came rolling in. Visions of graduation and studying to be a veterinarian danced in her head. She adored animals and wanted to dedicate her life to keeping them healthy.

But then God stepped in.

Working in the hearts of this sister trio (as only he can), he put Rebecca on bass, Alyssa on acoustic guitar, and Lauren on drums. Together they became BarlowGirl.

To the fans who look from the outside in, being on tour, recording a CD, talking about what God is doing in their lives, and sharing their biblical insights looks like a dream come true.

From the inside looking out, you get a slightly different picture.

Each member of this trio had to come to a place of surrender; a place of exchanging their agenda for God's; a place of saying, "Not my will, but your will be done"; a place of obedience, of stepping out in faith and going for it!

The girls all agreed, "God is strong in our weaknesses. He had a calling on our lives, and we couldn't ignore it."

So what has it been like? To their surprise, they've experienced fulfillment in using their gifts for God's purposes. What else have they received in exchange for their obedience?

"Complete contentment."

"Feeling God's joy and excitement."

"The desire to be only in God's will."

Alyssa adds, "This is what we were created for." Her sisters nodded.

---

**The Band:** "This is God's deal. We don't know how long it will last, but we just want to be in the center of his will. This is where his favor and his blessings come in."

**Clothes:** "It's hard to shop for modest clothes. That's why we're all about layering! With low rise [jeans] we have to have a long tank tucked in. We hold each other accountable by doing the bend test, the sit test, and the lean forward test. We don't want to have a "crack attack" in the middle of a show or while we're setting up. We're also careful not to have tops too tight."

**Purity:** "In a world that constantly bombards us with impurity and immodesty, we feel called to take a stand against what the world is telling us is acceptable, especially in the area of clothing and modesty."

# BARLOW BELIEFS

**Dating:** "We believe that God has one perfect man chosen for us; therefore, there's no need to worry about searching for him. When the time is right, God will bring us together. In the meantime, we can still be ourselves without the pressure of having to impress a guy. It's better to live without the pressure of having to have a boyfriend."

**Trust:** "We believe that God is calling everyone to live a life that is fully surrendered to him so that he can do his work in them and begin to show them his true purpose for their lives. We're definitely not saying 'we've mastered this concept, and now it's your turn,' but instead that this is a daily process and a journey that all of us will be on forever." *

* The girls shared these beliefs with me during a personal interview. Want more facts on BG? Head to www.barlowgirl.com.

# Curtain Call

"Do you believe in God?"

This was the fatal question asked in the library on the campus of Columbine High School on April 20, 1999. Cassie Bernall said yes. Rachel Scott said yes. Others said yes. Since you've read this far in this book, I'm hoping that you too would say yes. (Note: the question was not, Do you believe there is a God, but rather, Do you believe in God.)

Our God is a personal God. He's a living, breathing, heavenly Father who truly exists. And when you and I believe in him, our lives will show it.

Don't just sign up for the "fire insurance." I pray you aren't like some who hear the way of salvation through Jesus Christ and say yes just because they want to be saved from the punishment of their sin. They don't want to end up in hell, so they pray and accept Jesus as Savior. They choose to turn instead of burn, but they don't start walking! They don't change. They keep doing life their own way, totally ignoring the Bible's teachings and God's desires. They never make Jesus their Lord. They stay where they are and miss the most thrilling, exciting part of belonging to God's family and being a Christian.

Walking with God!

Living every day with him!

Hand in hand. Heart to heart. Breath by breath!

Totally God-conscious. He becomes your all in all!

To sum it up, is Jesus not just your Savior, but also your Lord? *Lord* means master, leader, authority. If you keep Jesus hanging on the sidelines of your life, you really won't care what his plans and purposes are for you. If he's your Lord, you'll recognize his position, submit to his will, obey his commandments, seek his counsel. In other words, his lordship in your life will show! So I'll ask again. Is Jesus your Lord?

## In Their Own Words . . .

You may never have to face the decision of whether or not to die for your faith, but every day you face the decision of whether or not you will live for it.*

~ DC Talk

* DC Talk nails it with this quote from their book *Jesus Freaks*, page 21.

# Lordship Countdown

Here are a bunch of statements that will help you sense exactly where you are with lordship. After reading the statement, write T for true or F for false on the blank space provided. Upon completion, tally up your T's and F's. See what happens!

_____ I feel uncomfortable at school when someone starts talking about God.

_____ I have a regular devotional time and really love it.

_____ I search the Bible to find answers and direction in my life.

_____ I listen for God's voice.

_____ I cringe when others tease me about being a Christian.

_____ I've seen positive changes in myself since I accepted Jesus.

_____ I secretly enjoy gossip.

_____ I obey my parents only when it's convenient for me.

_____ I control my language much better than I used to.

_____ I choose to dress in a way that reflects my body as God's temple.

_____ I have Christian friends.

_____ I make myself accountable to other believers.

_____ My greatest desire right now is to please and honor God.

_____ I'm eager to hear what God has to say to me.

_____ I often stop to ask myself, _What would Jesus do?_

_____ When I sense God is leading me in a direction I don't want to go, I eventually go his way even when I don't see his wisdom.

_____ I'm usually too busy or too tired to go to youth group.

_____ I love it when I serve others.

Add up your T's and F's:
_____ T's _____ F's

Are you satisfied with these results? Why or why not?

One of the ways you'll know whether Jesus is truly Lord over your life is if you think of asking him for direction first, before asking all your friends or even yourself. If you start to repeat a behavior that you know isn't right with God but then stop because you don't want to grieve your Jesus, then he's definitely the reigning King in your life. You discover that obedience brings you joy.

# The Unending
# ADVENTURE

There's one thing God will never stop asking you to do. He may ask you to do it in the morning, at noon, or at midnight! It may be in the school library, while you're at work, at the movies with friends, or in another country building a house for the poor.

Can you guess what that "one thing" is?

We're told to "go into all the world" and do what? Preach the gospel (Mark 16:15). Share the Good News of Jesus's death, burial, and resurrection! Tell people that forgiveness and eternal life in heaven are available to them today. They can have a personal relationship with the living God who created them and loves them. Nonbelievers matter to God.

This might be the single most eternally significant assignment ever. And it's given to you, to me, to everyone who calls Jesus "Lord" and God "Father." We've been given the ministry of reconciliation (2 Corinthians 5:18), meaning God wants you and me to be the spokespersons who draw people (mankind) back into a relationship with the Lord.

> Always be prepared to give an answer to everyone who asks you to give the reason for the hope that you have. But do this with gentleness and respect.
>
> 1 Peter 3:15 NIV

I don't want you to get caught not knowing what to say. That might make you feel guilty or ineffective. No need for that! Let's get prepared. You can check out specific tools for evangelism at www.navigators.org (click on "Ministry Tools," then click on "The Bridge to Life" and "One Verse Evangelism").

One thing that will help others be open to hearing about God is first knowing that you care about them. Develop a friendship with the people you feel the Holy Spirit is urging you to share with. Be approachable. Call them by their names. Initiate conversation. Ask open-ended questions so you can get to know them beyond a surface level. Really listen to their answers and maintain good eye contact.

It's a fact that 80 percent of people come to Christ through a friend. And 86 percent of people accept Jesus into their lives before the age of eighteen! That means you have the greatest chance of introducing your peers to Jesus right now! And when you do, be sure to celebrate! Throw a victory party! The Bible lets us in on a heavenly secret:

> There is rejoicing in the presence of the angels of God over one sinner who repents.
>
> Luke 15:10 NIV

Isn't God fun? He parties every time someone is born spiritually and becomes his child. Now, what should *you* do? Be her friend. Make sure she has a Bible. Pray with her. Invite her to church and youth group. Include her in a small group Bible study. Buy her a Christian CD.

Then do her the best favor ever! Explain to her that God created her and thinks she's **beautiful**. Tell her she doesn't have to do anything to make God like her—he **accepts** her and loves her with an unending love. Encourage her to identify the special abilities and spiritual gifts that God has **blessed** her with. Help her seek after the **eternally significant** plans that God has for her life. Show her she's a **B.A.B.E.**, just like you!

# THE B.A.B.E. CHECKLIST

Aren't you excited about all the different ways God can use you to do something eternally significant for his kingdom? It's especially valuable for you to grasp this stuff so that you never question your presence or purpose in this life. So let's see if you're tracking with me!

| Yes | No | Almost | |
|-----|-----|--------|---|
| _____ | _____ | _____ | I'm grasping the idea that life isn't all about me; it's all about the Lord. |
| _____ | _____ | _____ | I'm trusting God more and more as I read the Bible's examples of how he has used others for his purposes. |
| _____ | _____ | _____ | If a friend would ask me my purpose in life, I could explain it to her. |
| _____ | _____ | _____ | When I obey the Lord and accomplish the things on his to-do list for me, I'm being eternally significant and bringing glory to my heavenly Father. |
| _____ | _____ | _____ | I can do seemingly simple things in Jesus's name, and they become eternally significant. |
| _____ | _____ | _____ | The fact that I was created on purpose and for a purpose gets me excited to see what God is going to do in my life. |
| _____ | _____ | _____ | I can now set aside the world's superficial definition of significance and success because I understand God's definition: to discover his purposes for me and to do them! |
| _____ | _____ | _____ | When faced with a dilemma or a crossroads, I usually find myself consulting the Director and relying on his script. |
| _____ | _____ | _____ | I can see that God will match my spiritual gifts and natural abilities with the assignments he gives to me. |
| _____ | _____ | _____ | I'm evaluating my activities so I can have more time for God and his assignments. |
| _____ | _____ | _____ | I'm applying at least one of the study tips to help me dig into the script, the Bible. |

| Yes | No | Almost | |
|-----|-----|--------|---|
| _____ | _____ | _____ | I'm making a new effort to be sure that my spiritual life rules in every area of my life so I don't act differently at a party than I would at youth group. |
| _____ | _____ | _____ | I'm more aware of my need to be available, flexible, and faithful in my service to the Lord. |
| _____ | _____ | _____ | As I stay tight with the Lord, I'm studying, praying, listening, and watching to see where he's working, and I'm beginning to sense that I'm moving closer to understanding what God's starring role (purpose) is for me. |
| _____ | _____ | _____ | Jesus's lordship is showing in my life. |
| _____ | _____ | _____ | I'm awed at the fact that my life can bring glory to God. |
| _____ | _____ | _____ | I see that telling others how to have a personal relationship with Jesus is something God wants me to do, so I'm learning helpful tools for sharing the gospel with others. |
| _____ | _____ | _____ | I'm in a partnership with God. He alone knows my life's plan, yet I have to seek after him in order to discover what it is. |

# SHINE LIKE A

# B.A.

# B.E.!

# IT'S a WRaP!

Wow. Journeying through this book, we've learned a ton about God and about ourselves. (You learned while you read, and I learned while I wrote!) I pray you're changed. That you now see yourself the way your heavenly Father sees you. That you've clearly seen the truth in the Bible and know that what the world shoves at you is not reality, it's false. You aren't valued based on your looks. God doesn't compare you to others or judge you on your appearance. He loves what you see in the mirror. You're one hot divine diva, in heaven's opinion. Therefore, you can celebrate your look! You can focus on *being* beautiful since you already look beautiful.

I also pray that you're absorbing all the Scriptures that describe who you are in Christ. You don't have to perform or conform for the Lord to place his stamp of approval on you—you've already got it, just because you belong to him. Hopefully, you've made the big switch and are now living for an audience of One. His opinion of you is all that matters in the long run. Can you envision him cheering you on? He thinks you rock. He fully accepts you with no strings attached. Hopefully, this is helping you remember you don't have to bow to what others think you should do or be. You're free to be yourself!

Maybe one of your coolest discoveries has been that you're incredibly blessed. You're the proud owner of countless spiritual blessings that no one can take away from you. And you're gifted. Isn't it great to know that God's Spirit has personally selected the gifts you'll be using to fulfill God's plans for your life? By now you may have determined activities or ministries that your personality and spiritual gifts are ideal for. Since you have Holy Spirit power living in you, you can do whatever God asks you to do.

And doesn't it feel great to know you're here on earth, at this very time in history, for a reason? It's a fact! Your life isn't about nothingness. It's all about being eternally significant for the Lord! As you stay tight with your Maker, you'll continually see what you were made to do. Your spiritual gifts, special abilities, personality, and passions will all work together in the role God alone has written just for you. There are no understudies for this! You alone can do what God has prepared.

Girlfriend, you are **beautiful**, you are **accepted**, you are **blessed**, and you are **eternally significant**! You are a **B! A! B! E!** And what does it spell? **B.A.B.E.!** Don't ever forget it.

May I pray for you?

Heavenly Father, Thank you that my young friend reading this book is doing so by divine appointment. You wanted her to read it to learn that she's a B.A.B.E.! Show her over and over that she's incredibly **beautiful** in your eyes, she's **accepted** by you just the way she is, and you love her so much that you want to help her become her very best. Thank you for showering her with so many **blessings**—help her to be a grateful girl! Keep her tuned in and trusting that you do have a plan for her life, a plan that is **eternally significant**! Strengthen her, Lord, to be obedient to follow your ways and remind her that when she feels like she's standing alone, she's not. You are always with her. And above all, Father, open her eyes to your unending love for her.

I ask this in Jesus's name, amen!

**You were created on purpose and for a purpose. Go live like it, B.A.B.E.!**

# Catch the B.A.B.E. Wave

There are teen girls all over the globe who are reading this book and catching the B.A.B.E. wave! They're discovering that they're B.A.B.E.s in God's eyes, in his opinion, in his kingdom! And ultimately, that's **all** that matters. There are girls just like you who want to honor God with their lives and live out his purposes for them.

The B.A.B.E. wave is on the move! And you can help keep it rolling.

Now that you understand that you're a B.A.B.E., you can help other girls discover that they too are beautiful, accepted, blessed, and eternally significant. You can skyrocket their self-esteem by chatting up the fact that they were created *on* purpose and *for* a purpose.

Wherever you live, whatever your life situation, you can start right now to shape your generation by giving them a crystal clear vision of who they are in Christ and what they're here on earth to do. Life isn't meaningless—not even sorta! Pray for opportunities to tell others—cousins, classmates, teammates, co-workers. Pray for the right words at the right time. Pray for listeners' hearts to be open. And pray for your B.A.B.E. girlfriends around the world to remember **who they are** and to be courageous, knowing that God is with them as they take their message to their peers.

Live the B.A.B.E. message. Share the B.A.B.E. message. Keep the B.A.B.E. wave rolling.

I'll be praying for **you**!

# Confirm Your B.A.B.E. Status!

Let's make it official. If you've read this entire book and are ready to declare yourself a B.A.B.E.—now and forever—then sign on the dotted line.

I, _____, truly believe that I am beautiful in my heavenly Father's eyes. I am accepted by him unconditionally. I am blessed with spiritual gifts and special abilities that he chose for me. I am eternally significant with a life plan that will make a difference. I am a B.A.B.E.

I choose to develop God-Beauty. I choose to have an audience of One and to see my value based upon what God's Word says about me. I choose to develop and use my gifts and talents for God's purposes. I choose to seek God's plan for my life so that I will be eternally significant and will bring him glory.

I choose to become the kind of young woman God can use. I choose to be the B.A.B.E. that I am.

Signature: _____
Date: _____

# Be a B.A.B.E. in Action!
## THE ULTIMATE SPA EXPERIENCE

Can you already smell the fragrant aroma of fresh lavender, the sweet scent of French vanilla, or maybe soothing peppermint? Perhaps fruity berry or tantalizing tangerine is more what you have in mind. The scent of your spa day can't hold a candle to the fragrant aroma of Christ that will fill the air!

*What is she babbling about?*

I'm talking about you and your cool group of B.A.B.E.s banding together to do something totally . . . well . . . babe-a-licious!

That's right. You're going to have the opportunity to put the main points of being a B.A.B.E. into action. You're going to feel stunningly beautiful as you do something wonderful for others, share your glowing confidence that comes from being totally accepted, and use the special abilities and spiritual gifts you've been blessed with to pull together an event that will bless others. And you'll be living out part of the Lord's eternally significant plan for your life.

Intrigued? Good! Ready for a challenge and a very fun time? Attagirl! I'll fill in the details using who, what, where, when, why, and how.

## Who

You, your sister B.A.B.E.s, your youth leaders or moms (you might *not* need their help but they're great to have around to wipe up the spills, clean up the mess, make your refreshments—you know, that kind of stuff), and your very special guests: the older and wonderfuler (nope, not a word) women in your church! This will be a character-building experience for you and a bonding experience between you and some church members who often feel left out or forgotten. You're going to bring a spark of life to some elderly and widowed ladies who share your love for Jesus.

## What

The ultimate spa experience! Everyone needs a bit of pampering—

especially those who live alone or who don't get out much. Not only will you show love and kindness to them on spa day, but you'll get to continue it when you see them at church. About the day: you can choose to offer several spa services at your B.A.B.E. Salon for Seniors (manicures, pedicures, facials, makeup, shoulder and neck massages) or choose one specialty of the day (manicures with massage of the hands and forearm). That part is up to you. Just your smile, touch, and giving of your time will light up these women's lives (and put a smile on your Father's face).

### Where

Set up your spa at church—everyone already knows how to get there. Get permission from your church to use a room with a sink and a microwave nearby. If you expect only a few women, then doing it in a home is great. If you have a few willing (and safe) drivers, offer a pick-up service for those who can't drive.

### When

As soon as you can! Well, okay, it takes some planning and prayer. Select a date and time; then get it on the church calendar. Prepare and pass out or send out invitations. Designate a person the attendees call to make their appointment or take sign-ups at church. If you're open from 1:00 to 4:00 p.m., give an approximate time. For instance, between 2:00 p.m. and 2:30 p.m. Depending on the number of B.A.B.E.s helping, remember that you can schedule more than one person at a time. You just don't want fifty ladies showing up at the same time.

### Why

I added this one as a pop quiz. By now you really, really, really should know why. So go ahead. Answer this question yourself:

### How

Most of this is up to you. I'll give you some suggestions, but make this something your group plans together. Think pamper, pamper, pamper! The main goal isn't that your guests leave with perfect looking nails or makeup but that they know they're loved! So here we go.

**Brainstorm!** Think through the details of your day, make a list of the various things that need to be done, and then divvy them up amongst the B.A.B.E.s according to their special abilities, talents, and spiritual gifts. Let the artists decorate, the organizers advertise, the servants clean the spa room, the teachers make Scripture notes for the ladies to take home, the intercessors pray, the encouragers make party favors (individually wrapped polish remover pads would be great), the domestic girls make tasty finger foods, and so on.

**Get the word out!** Design invitations and posters to be mailed or passed out at church. Talk it up.

**Gather Supplies!** Depending on what you choose to do, you need to secure your supplies. For instance, for manicures you'll need a hand towel or cloth placemat for the women to lay their hands on, scented lotions for massaging hands/forearms, a bowl of warm soapy water for soaking cuticles, nail clippers (rinse with alcohol between uses), emery boards for filing, wooden orange sticks for pushing back cuticles, and cotton pads. You'll need several bottles of base coat/top coat, a selection of

nail polishes, and polish remover for goofs. Perhaps while they wait their turn you could wrap their hands in warm, damp washcloths. Based on what you plan to offer your guests, round up what you need.

**Tongue Tied!** Not! Make the women feel valued by talking to them! You can chat it up easily enough with your gal pals, but what about a B.A.B.E. four or five times your age? Get your juices flowing and create a list of questions so no one gets brain freeze!

## Go for It!

Okay, that's it. Please email me at andrea@andreastephens.com with the details of how it all turned out. Naturally, if you want to do something completely different you can—just be sure you are applying your B.A.B.E. identity to the event. Then, email me about what you did—I may want it for my website! Go shine, B.A.B.E.!

# THE B.A.B.E. "CHAT IT UP" GUIDE

Whether you're hanging with your friends from school or your small group from church, here are some questions that will spark some conversation and get you all abuzz about the things you've learned about being a true B.A.B.E.! As you share your insights and opinions, as your friends chat about theirs, you'll all benefit and learn from each other. This isn't a pop quiz kind of thing, so no, you don't *have* to talk about every question. I do suggest grabbing a notebook or journal to track your answers. So give it a go and see what else you can squeeze out of this book about your new life as a B.A.B.E.!

### B Is for Beautiful!

1. In your own words, define *beautiful*. How can you *feel* beautiful?
2. Like Sarah, when have you been teased about your appearance? How did you respond? Do you believe you can have the confidence Sarah had because she understood she was gorgeous in God's sight?
3. God designed each of us with a custom-designed look. How do you feel when our culture tries to dictate to you how you need to look? Share what you love about each other's appearance (like favorite feature).
4. Have you ever caught yourself judging others solely based on their outer appearance? God doesn't have a rating system, and he sees each of us as equally gorgeous. Describe how this can help you be less judgmental.
5. How would your thoughts (*I hate my curly hair, My hips are so huge*, etc.) and actions (dieting, clothing, body

language) change if you were really content with your physical design?

6. You're in line to pay for your Wild Cherry Diet Pepsi when you notice a rack full of magazines with picture-perfect models staring at you. Now that you've read "B Is for Beautiful!" what are your analytical thoughts about what you see?

7. Reread "The Perfect Body." Do you have a perfect body according to this perspective?

8. Describe the two dangerous attitudes that result from comparing yourself to other girls. Which attitude have you struggled with the most?

9. What is your opinion of a person (especially a teen) getting an extreme makeover?

10. You have the power to choose to let others' rude comments or uncalled-for actions either penetrate your soul or roll off your back. So how are you going to react?

11. Of the seven steps for achieving God-Beauty, which have you done? Which are you working on? Which had you never considered before as being part of beauty?

12. Choose two Scriptures from this section to memorize. What are they?

### A Is for Accepted!

1. In your own words, define *accepted*.

2. What negative behaviors have you fallen into in an attempt to be wanted, noticed, or accepted?

3. Understanding God's unconditional acceptance gives you a sense of freedom to be yourself, a sense of belonging, and a sense of security. How does each of these things make a difference in your everyday life, in your future hopes and dreams?

4. It's a fact that not every person you want to have accept you actually will. So what should you do?

5. You are known, included, valued, and loved by God. What is your heart's response to this truth? What does it do to your confidence level?

6. Identify a situation when no one applauded you. How did you feel? How would it have been different if you had an audience of One? List the benefits of this solo audience.

7. How can you respond with gentleness and kindness when a family member trashes you?

8. What does it mean to be "in Christ"? One at a time, read aloud each of the thirty-eight "in Christ" statements, replacing the words "you are" with "I am." How does that rock you? Now share your favorite truth from the above list and explain why.

9. What does it take to be a frapuccino flop? Which of the eleven descriptions sounds like something you (or a friend) have done in your personal search for acceptance?

10. In what ways are you currently facing raunchy rejection? How did Jesus respond to it? List some positive ways to handle it.

11. One of the suggestions in "Blast Out the Blues" is to pay attention to your self-talk (you know, the things you say in your private thoughts). Choose to turn them around. Negative to positive. Bad to good. Give examples of doing this.

12. Choose two Scriptures from this section to memorize. What are they?

### B Is for Blessed!

1. You guessed it—in your own words define *blessed*. What makes a blessing spiritual?

2. What does Jesus mean to you? What are you doing in hopes that others will see Jesus in you?

3. Forgiveness! It's almost an unexplainable blessing. But go ahead and try. Without the blessings of forgiveness in your life, where might you be?

4. Hey, divine diva, the Holy Spirit lives inside of you! You're housing holiness. How does that bit of info affect the way you live your day-to-day life or how you treat your body?

5. Describe the six purposes of the Holy Spirit. Which one are you most thankful for and why?

6. Define the Spirit's nine qualities that get us glowing from the inside out. Which one do you need the most today?

7. Jesus is the Vine, and you are the branch! What can happen if you disconnect from the Vine?

8. What are your spiritual gifts, and what has helped you define them? How have you seen your (or a friend's) spiritual gift in action? Why does God want you to develop them?

9. What are some important things to remember when you're struggling to believe that God has everything under control?

10. Describe a kaleidoscope blessing in your life—something that you can look back on and see how the pieces fit to create a beautiful picture.

11. Why is it important to understand the difference between giving thanks *for* all things and giving thanks *in* all things? Ultimately, who decides your daily outlook on life? Explain.

12. Choose two Scriptures from this section to memorize. Write them in your blessings book.

### *E Is for Eternally Significant!*

1. By now you know the drill—in your own words define *eternally significant*.

2. What temporary kind of stuff do you see you and your friends being easily wrapped up in?

3. God's plan for you involves teamwork! What's God's part? What's yours? Is there anything you need to do to play your part better?

4. Describe a woman you think is significant. What's the key to her success or impact? I defined the true meaning of success as discovering God's purpose for you and doing it. Do you agree? Why or why not?

5. Wow! The whole servant idea is so opposite of our culture. Describe a true servant attitude and how you can serve your family in the coming week.

6. What questions might drag you down the wrong path for your life? What are the right questions, and how can they make the difference?

7. Do you have a horror story about an audition? Share it with your group, then rate each other's stories. Whose wins hands down? What does it mean to you that God doesn't hold auditions?

8. You're a star with a part that's been written just for you. How will you go about discovering and training for it? Now mix your spiritual gifts, your natural abilities, and your personality. Shake it up and what might you become? What can you see yourself doing for God?

9. How can you make your day-to-day opportunities and activities count for eternity (at school, at work, at home, etc.)?

10. How can giving up your agenda and going with God's plan be an act of worship? What might the results of this be?

11. The big guy wearing his football jersey just walked by and dropped this on you: "You're such a stinkin' goody-goody." What's your response?

12. Choose two Scriptures from this section to memorize. What are they?

# THE B.A.B.E. "CHAT IT UP" LEADER'S GUIDE

Congratulations, B.A.B.E.! You've agreed to be a student or adult leader for a group of teen girls (or you're praying about it, and I'm hoping you're going to go for it). Do you know what that makes you? (No, crazy is *not* the right answer!) It makes you a brave, totally awesome, and absolutely obedient B.A.B.E.! Cool!

I've personally witnessed the phenomenon that takes place when a group of girls get together to talk (one of their favorite pastimes). Eventually their walls come down and their hearts open up. How special that you get to be a part of that. What exactly is your role? First, it's just caring enough to *have* the group, meeting consistently, and bringing some munchies. But it's way more than that. Your group needs your presence, your wisdom, and your walk with God lived out in front of

them. Your job isn't to lecture them (they have moms for that). Instead, you have the opportunity to provide a safe and nurturing setting where they can learn from each other, the Bible, and the information collected for them in this book. You get to encourage them to give an honest response to the "Chat It Up" questions and to apply the truths they discover to their personal lives. To all this add your own life experiences, and you've got "good soil" for growing the next generation of godly B.A.B.E.s!

Sounds like a tall order, huh? Relax! You're the leader, but the Holy Spirit is the teacher! John 14:26 reminds us, "The Counselor, the Holy Spirit, whom the Father will send in my name, will teach you all things" (NIV). Ultimately, the Spirit of God teaches the girls, and he even helps you lead! You don't do it alone. Whew!

## Andrea's Top 10 Guidelines for Leading a Chat Session

Here are some tips for enhancing your time with your group:

1. **Pray!** Pray for God's guidance as you prepare and share. Pray for each girl in your group. Pray

that the eyes of her heart would be enlightened so she would know the hope of her calling (Ephesians 1:18). Pray that she would be filled with the knowledge of God's will in all spiritual wisdom and understanding so that she may walk in a manner worthy of the Lord, pleasing him in all areas of her life and bearing fruit in every good work she attempts for the Lord (Colossians 1:9–10). For those who don't know the Lord, pray that they would see their need for him and say yes to his saving grace.

2. **Be prepared!** Read through the entire book; then go back and prepare each week by reviewing the section and answering the "Chat It Up" questions. Be willing to share one personal story that relates to the topic of the week, yet be sensitive to the amount of time you talk about you! One or two stories can help your group open up, but too many stories may make them feel you don't want to hear about them! Balance is always the key!

3. **Welcome them!** This works best when you're the first one to arrive at the meeting spot (church, Starbucks, a restaurant). Get some tunes going, mix up some lemonade, and be ready so that when they walk through the door, your attention is on them.

4. **Encourage participation!** The first few weeks, allow your group to participate at their own comfort level. Everyone need not answer every question. Eventually it will be good if each girl shares. After all, this book is all about girls' issues—things they deal with and things they have opinions on! For those shy B.A.B.E.s, rather than just calling on them, which puts them on the spot, go for a gentler approach (instead of "Melissa, your turn" try "We would love to hear how you answered that question, Melissa. Would you be willing to share?"). Now, for the girl who always has something to say and is the first one to say it, bring along some duct tape. Just kidding! Try something like, "Sarah, we like hearing your answers, but let's have someone else go first this time." Hopefully, that will help! **Important:** Every answer matters! No response is too insignificant. Do your best to validate and affirm their answers.

5. **Be genuine!** Ask questions with interest and warmth. Maintain as much eye contact with the group

as possible (especially with the one who's talking). Be conscious of your facial expressions and body language (smiling is good, nodding off is bad).

6. **Go deeper!** If you want them to elaborate on an answer or you don't quite understand what they're saying, try phrases like, "Tell us more about that." "Why do you feel that way?" "How did that make you feel?" "What did you learn from that situation?" "What would you do differently next time?" "When you say _____, what does that mean to you?"

7. **Be creative!** Add visual aids like magazine ads, movie clips, props, posters, book excerpts, skits, role playing, and more! Use your imagination. It keeps the learning fun for you and them!

8. **Let the Spirit lead!** Commit each week to the Lord. If the lesson seems to be going in a different direction or if your group seems intense on one aspect of the lesson, be willing to forgo the plan, trusting that the Spirit wants to do a work in the girls' lives right then. It's important to discern between the Holy Spirit's direction, a rabbit trail, and one girl getting on her soap box! But if there's sin-

cere interaction, go with it. There might even be someone who becomes visibly upset or tearful. Feel free to stop to pray for her. Follow up by asking her if there's anything she needs or if there's anything you can do to help.

9. **Welcome silence!** I realize that five seconds can feel like five hours when you toss out a question and suddenly no one has a thing to say! Don't panic—allow them time to process the question and think about their answer. If necessary, reword the question and toss it out again.

10. **Be brave!** Two thoughts here. First, in a group of teen girls, there will be differences of opinion, levels of experience, and spiritual maturity. Allow for it and expect it. Do your best to highlight answers that are closest to the biblical point of view. Second, there are bound to be questions you can't answer. There may even be someone in the group who actually gets a kick out of trying to stump you! Believe me, I've been there. I encourage you to turn it into a positive and congratulate them for really thinking hard! It shows they're hungry for truth. Write down the question and do your best to have an

answer the next week. You might even challenge the group to search their Bibles ( "What does the Bible say about wisdom?" ) or poll girls at school ( "What percentage of girls really think it's possible to be a virgin when they get married?" ) so that you can dig for the answer together.

## *Playing by the Rules!*

Here are some simple rules to share with your small group:

~ Keep it confidential. What's shared in the group stays in the group.
~ Avoid judging. Respect the views of others.
~ Don't fix it. Offer advice only if it's requested.
~ No interrupting. Whoever's speaking, let her finish.
~ Take turns. Don't do all the talking. We learn more by listening.
~ Pray for group members. It's the kindest and most powerful thing you can do.

## *Getting Started!*

Secure a copy of *Girlfriend, You Are a B.A.B.E.* for each participant. Have pens/pencils, Bibles, and extra paper handy. Have a sign-in sheet—include name, address, phone number, and email address. Challenge yourself to memorize the girls' names ASAP. Personally contacting them a few times during the course of the study means the world to them. Send a note or an email or give them a call. If you have more than ten girls, recruit another leader and have two groups. Feel free to add or delete some of the "Chat It Up" questions. You know your group best. Focus in on their needs.

## *Try This Lineup!*

~ Hey, Glad You're Here! (Greet Them)
~ Get Those Pretty Little Heads Thinking! (General Opening Question)
~ Invite Jesus to Join You! (Opening Prayer)
~ What's God Up To? (Praise Reports/Testimonies)
~ Hide It in Your Heart! (Memory Verse)
~ And the Answer Is . . . ! ( "Chat It Up" Q & A)
~ Change and Rearrange! (Personal Application)
~ Wrap It Up! (Closing Prayer)
~ What's Up Next Week! (Assignment and Memory Verse)

BEAUTIFUL

# The B.A.B.E. Event

### Beautiful - Accepted - Blessed - Eternally Significant®

ETERNALLY SIGNIFICANT®

The B.A.B.E Event

FEATURING:

# Andrea Stephens

> The B.A.B.E. Event™ Creator   > Former Wilhelmina Model, NYC
> Author: *Girlfriend, You Are a B.A.B.E.!, Stuff a Girl's Gotta Know, Boyland, Bible B.A.B.E.S, Glamour Girls,* and more!
> *Brio* Magazine Beauty Editor   > check out www.andreastephens.com

## a teen girl event

### Event Includes:
Great topics, workbook, makeup samples, giveaways, fashion trends, music, drama & special guests!

### For More Info:
> Call toll free 1-866-907-BABE (2223)
> Go to www.andreastephens.com for event locations & info on bringing The B.A.B.E. Event™ to your area!
> Email Andrea Stephens at andrea@andreastephens.com

### We'll Chat About:
Becoming a Real B.A.B.E.™
Loving Your Look
Fresh Confidence
Discovering Your Spiritual Gifts & Talents
Defining Your Passion & Purpose

Find us on Facebook!

BLESSED